Praise for *The Shibumi Strategy*

"This is a treasure of a book, and just the kind of uplifting medicine that's needed right now. It's about something that in the west we don't even have a name for, and yet it holds the key to finding our way in challenging times. When you know how to look at the events of your life, everything is there to show you what you can't see on your own, and offer you opportunities that you normally walk right by. No matter your life circumstances, this is the kind of book that can (and almost certainly will) change your life."

—**Sarah Susanka,** author, *The Not So Big Life* and *The Not So Big House* series

"*The Shibumi Strategy* is a simple but affecting tale—a must-read for anyone looking to make sense of breakthrough change at work and in life."

—**Ori Brafman,** coauthor, *Click: The Magic of Instant Connections*

the shibumi strategy

a powerful way to create MEANINGFUL CHANGE

matthew e. may

a personal leadership fable

JOSSEY-BASS
A Wiley Imprint
www.josseybass.com

Published by Jossey-Bass
A Wiley Imprint
989 Market Street, San Francisco, CA 94103-1741—www.josseybass.com

Jossey-Bass books and products are available through most bookstores. To contact Jossey-
Bass directly call our Customer Care Department within the U.S. at 800-956-7739, outside
the U.S. at 317-572-3986, or fax 317-572-4002.

Jossey-Bass also publishes its books in a variety of electronic formats. Some content that
appears in print may not be available in electronic books.

Library of Congress Cataloging-in-Publication Data
May, Matthew E.
    The shibumi strategy : a powerful way to create meaningful change /
Matthew E. May.—1st ed.
        p. cm.
    Includes bibliographical references.
    ISBN 978-0-470-76950-8 (cloth); ISBN 978-0-470-89214-5 (ebk);
    ISBN 978-0-470-89215-2 (ebk); ISBN 978-0-470-89216-9 (ebk)
    1. Commitment (Psychology) 2. Zen Buddhism. I. Title.
    BF619.M39 2010
    158—dc22

                                                    2010025176

Printed in the United States of America
FIRST EDITION
HB Printing   10 9 8 7 6 5 4 3 2 1

To Deva, Kendal, Koreen, and Morgan,
may the spirit of shibumi always inhabit
heart, mind, body, and soul.

To my father,
who taught me at an early age that
"all things change, and we must change with them."

Though a thousand times a thousand men are conquered by one in battle, the one who conquers himself is truly the master of battle.

—GAUTAMA BUDDHA

contents

the shibumi strategy

introduction

There are times in life when if fortunate we experience a moment of utter clarity. We feel wide awake and connected and balanced: everything makes sense, we know exactly who we are, what we want, and why we're here. In that moment, be it one blink or a thousand, our effectiveness is maximal. And yet our actions seem minimal, effortless even, and the experience is consummately satisfying.

These are breakthrough moments.

There is an ineffable quality to these experiences. Some have tried to define and describe them using English terms—such as *zone* and *flow*—that are inadequate to capture the essence of the moment, mostly because they simply compare the feeling to something known yet ultimately inferior, or express merely some part of the whole.

These are moments of *shibumi.*

Shibumi is a Japanese word, the meaning of which is reserved for just these kinds of experiences.

1

With roots in the Zen aesthetic ideals of art, architecture, and gardening, it is used in a wide variety of contexts, and has come to denote those things that exhibit in paradox and all at once the very best of everything and nothing: Elegant simplicity. Effortless effectiveness. Understated excellence. Beautiful imperfection.

James Michener referred to shibumi in his 1968 novel *Iberia*, writing that it can't be translated and has no explanation. Soetsu Yanagi in his 1972 book *The Unknown Craftsman* talked about shibumi in the context of art, writing that a true work of art is one whose intentionally imperfect beauty makes an artist of the viewer. The author Trevanian (the nom de plume of Dr. Rodney William Whitaker) wrote in his 1979 best-selling novel *Shibumi*, "*Shibumi* has to do with great refinement underlying commonplace appearances."

Sometimes these moments of shibumi register in our consciousness. Yet when they do, we don't really search for an explanation, think about a deeper meaning, learn from them, or even give thought to how we might extend the experience.

What if we are constantly being sent signals and offered opportunities, but because we are so involved in our mad rush to survive the day, we simply don't receive them? What if we're stuck, asleep at the wheel, and we just don't know it, because our conventional ways of thinking, rigidly structured routines, and solidly set minds block us from discovering what the universe is calling us to do?

And what if there was a way for us to actually engineer some sort of personal process that lets us break through those barriers and discover how to live a life in pursuit of shibumi?

One way to answer these questions is to examine more closely the events that direct us this way and that, treat them as learning moments in order to draw lessons from them, and then think about the kinds of steps to take and connections to make—in our work, in our personal lives—that might precipitate a breakthrough and put us on the path in pursuit of shibumi.

Perhaps this simple fable helps shed some light. While it is purely a work of fiction, the story is an amalgam of real experiences, some relayed to me over the years by friends and family, others of my own (I became familiar with the various concepts supporting the pursuit of shibumi over the course of an eight-year engagement with a

Japanese company). And although the events are fictional, the philosophies, principles, and practices revealed in the story are quite real, grounded in both ancient Eastern philosophy and current Western neuroscience.

With any luck, it will touch a universal chord while enabling you to find your own uniquely personal interpretation.

the
fable

the commitment

Until one is committed, there is hesitancy, the chance to draw back, always
ineffectiveness. The moment one definitely commits oneself, then
providence moves too. All sorts of things occur to help one that would
never otherwise have occurred. A whole stream of events issues
from the decision, raising in one's favor all manner of unforeseen incidents,
meetings and material assistance which no man could have
dreamed would have come his way.

−W. H. MURRAY

The news wasn't good. In fact, to Andy Harmon,
it couldn't have been any worse. Rumblings that
Mega Box Electronics was moving its customer
service call center out of Twin Falls, in fact out of
the country, had been circulating through the company grapevine for weeks. Some people thought it
was inevitable, given the dismal state of the national
economy and the accompanying cost-cutting measures, like outsourcing, that large companies were
taking. Still, Mega Box wasn't in serious financial
difficulty the way many big corporations were, at

least not yet, and most thought it wouldn't happen. When it did, the 150 telephone sales and service representatives and 10 managers who received the rather distant memo from Mega Box headquarters in their final paychecks that Friday morning were in a state of shock. Andy was among them.

"Effective Immediately," the memo read. That meant grab a cardboard carton, clear out your personal belongings, and do not report to work come Monday morning. Andy sat in his small office watching things fold up and fall apart. Everyone was dazed and confused. His team of fifteen associates alternated between packing up and glancing his way for some sort of sign or guidance. The sad part was that he had none to offer. Shaking his head and shrugging his shoulders in a faint-hearted attempt at empathy only made matters worse.

I'm just no help at all, he thought.

Andy moved like a robot as he packed his own boxes. It didn't take very long, and when he finished, he sat down for the last time at his desk. He massaged his temples, rubbed his eyes, and pinched the bridge of his nose, trying to make his sudden headache go away. He couldn't quite describe the feeling, but part-panic and part-paralysis came pretty close. The walk from his office to his car was the longest of his life. Later, he wouldn't even remember all the handshakes, good-byes, and apologies.

Andy drove the short distance home as if on autopilot. The familiar tree-lined streets and storefronts and neighborhoods of Twin Falls were one big blur. Pulling into his driveway before noon felt strange, the empty house seemed foreign, and he was at a complete loss as he walked into the kitchen and poured himself a glass of water. He was thankful that no one was home, that the kids were at school. He needed time to think.

I have no idea what I'm going to do.

Besides Mega Box, Twin Falls didn't exactly have a lot to offer in the way of jobs. Most of its industry, if you could call it that, was somehow related to agriculture or printing. Twin Falls was in the center of a fertile lower Midwestern valley. There were a number of large flower and tree farms, supplying major retail nurseries. Produce growers dotted the valley floor, as did sheep and cattle farms. There were even a few local vineyards. There were a few low-cost printing plants, and then the typical mix of small shops and necessities: markets, salons, professional services, and the *Twin Falls Sentinel*, the weekly newspaper. Until that day, the biggest story for the *Sentinel* had been when Mega Box Electronics had broken ground on a national call center facility nearly ten years prior. Today's announcement of the closing would now lay claim to the record for biggest feature.

The questions began running through Andy's head. *What in the world will I do for work? Will we have to move? I'm forty-seven, f'goshsakes—what am I to do? How will my family take the news?*

Calm down, he thought, *take a breath*. He walked outside to the small deck he'd built two summers ago, and which had now become a favorite family gathering place when the weather was good. The deck looked out over a shallow slope that led to the woods that edged their property. Andy often sat out there; the peacefulness had a calming effect on him. As he sat trying to clear his thoughts, something his father once told him popped into his head: *"Two kinds of people in the world, Andrew. Those who let things happen, and those who make things happen. Be the second kind."*

Andy and his wife, Lizzy, had moved to Twin Falls eight years ago to escape the mad dash of the urban scene.

They had been the quintessential modern professional couple, living in Chicago. Andy had progressed up the ranks to regional sales manager for a global pharmaceuticals corporation. Lizzy had been the science editor for an academic publishing company. Neither of them saw Chicago as the ideal place to raise a family, so they investigated the country living scene, finally settling on Twin Falls, several hundred miles southwest of downtown Chicago. Mega Box had just announced its facility, and with Andy's sales background, the opportunity to manage the center seemed like a perfect fit. They had fallen in love with what they called "their little acre of heaven," and soon put down deep roots in the small community. Lizzy was now the volunteer high school librarian. Both of their children had been born in the Twin Falls Hospital. Scotty was now nearly eight years old, and Sandra, five, had just started school.

Now this.

What are my options? Andy thought as he sat staring out at the woods. *Do I even have any? Yes, of course, there are always options. Think.*

Andy had a way with people and liked connecting with others, that much he knew. It seemed to energize him. Sales had provided him a great way to live out his role as a "people person." It was the relationship-building part that he really liked, not so much the deal transaction part.

That's as good a place to start as any, he said almost out loud. He immediately found a notepad and pencil and began scratching out possibilities. The physical movement of taking action, any action, felt good.

Unfortunately, the list was short, assuming that they were going to stay in the area. The nearest same-size town to Twin Falls was fifty-five miles further south, with the one decent road there being an old two-laner, and no real industry to speak of either. As far as Andy could see, there were only two choices: stay in Twin Falls or move back to Chicago. He knew moving back would change their lives dramatically, and not for the better. Moving back meant moving backward.

The only place he knew of that might be hiring was Mainstreet Motors, the town's only car dealership, which sold new and used cars of all makes, models, and brands. He winced at the idea, an instinctive reaction, remembering his two experiences buying cars there.

But he had to try. He couldn't move his family away from their dream. The last thing he wanted to do was deliver frightening news. *I lost my job today and I don't know what we're going to do.* He simply could not face them empty-handed. For everyone's sake, if he had to tell them about Mega Box shutting down, he needed something, anything, to grab on to—something that gave them all a little bit of hope and assurance that things would be all right. It didn't need to be perfect. It just needed to *be*.

Andy made up his mind on the spot: *We're staying. I've got to get a job, today.*

He grabbed his keys and headed back out the door, determined to land work before the day was through.

As Andy pulled into the customer parking of Mainstreet Motors, he noticed the band of salesmen gathered outside the front door. He knew them all by name. *Fortunes of a small town*, he thought.

"Jerry. Bill. Mike," he muttered, nodding as he walked straight past them as quickly as he could.

"You buyin' today, Andy?" asked Bill. The others instantly shot Bill a warning look. They had heard the news. Bill hadn't.

"What?" Bill shrugged.

Andy ignored him. "Which way is Grady's office?" he asked, to no one in particular. Grady Carver was the general sales manager, and one of the first people Andy had met when he moved to Twin Falls.

> When you have decided what you believe, what you feel must be done, have the courage to stand alone and be counted.
>
> —ELEANOR ROOSEVELT

"Through the showroom, upstairs, left corner," replied Mike. "Good luck," he said, knowingly.

Andy headed toward Grady's office, not knowing exactly what he was going to say or do. He saw Grady through the glass wall, just hanging up the phone. As he was about to knock, Grady glanced up and waved him in.

"Andy Harmon! Howyadoinhowzitgoingoodtasee ya! Long time no see!" He smiled, adding, "What can I do you for?" Grady had that certain confident salesman-like quality about him, all smiles, all the time.

14

Andy motioned to the chair. "Hi, Grady, do you mind if I sit?"

"Not at all," answered Grady, motioning to the empty director's chairs facing his desk. "What can I help you with?"

"Might as well cut right to the chase," Andy replied. "You heard about Mega Box shutting down, right?"

Grady nodded. He had heard the rumors. And he didn't like the news. It would hurt sales, he figured.

"Effective today," confirmed Andy.

"Man, that's rough." Grady's face took on a rare frown, somewhat exaggerated.

Andy nodded back, looking Grady in the eyes. "Which is why I'm here. I have a hunch that most of the Mega Box folks are going to be leaving. I'm not. My family is staying put. So I'm asking you, can you use another salesman?"

Grady sat back, thinking, appraising Andy. He hooked his hands into his belt, then took them out again and leaned forward, resting his forearms on the desk and lacing his fingers together in that rigid way people do when they're delivering bad news or explaining something difficult in a serious way.

"Honestly, no," Grady began. "Correction . . . I can't use another man in sales, but I can always use another *great* salesman. Times aren't as good as they used to be. Cars aren't exactly flying off the lot. The sales team is already lean as it is. Adding another body might not be the best idea."

Andy remained silent, nodding his understanding of Grady's predicament.

"Look, Andy," Grady went on, "I know you're a professional. Sales manager at Mega Box, and all. But this business is tough. It's totally different. And it's not that I couldn't use a star player down there, but the question is, are you really up for it? You ever sold cars before? And what happens when something better comes along for you—what am I supposed to do?"

Andy took in Grady's answer, then countered it. "The most important thing to me is staying here, making sure things are steady and stable for my family. I'll commit myself to doing whatever it takes, for however long it takes me. I'm asking for the opportunity, that's all."

Grady sat back again. *Not a bad answer*, he thought.

"Hmm . . . It's a commission-only deal, you know that, right?" Grady said. "And the benefits don't kick

16

in for ninety days, and then only if you hit your number on a regular basis."

"You're saying it's up to me to make things happen," said Andy. "I can live with that."

"Tell you what," Grady offered, "I'll give you a month, trial basis. On-the-job training, no favors. You gotta be selling two a week by this time next month. I've got a business to run here. Mind you, you make a go of it, and you can make a damned good living here. Sell five a week, you're living large in Twin Falls. No easy challenge, though. One, maybe two guys have ever done that. Yours truly being one.

"Game?" asked Grady, standing and extending his hand.

"Game," confirmed Andy, taking it.

"Good." Grady smiled. "You're here bell to bell, starting tomorrow. Saturday's our biggest day. Trial by fire, baby. Be here early, 7:30 sharp."

"Thanks, Grady. I appreciate this, really. Means a lot to me. You don't even know."

Grady waved him off. "Yeah, yeah, what do they always say? Be careful what you wish for? See you in the morning. Bright and early."

Andy left Grady's office, and walking back through the showroom, he saw the entire sales team occupied, busy on the phones, heads down.

17

If you don't make a total commitment to whatever you're doing, then you start looking to bail out the first time the boat starts leaking. It's tough enough getting that boat to shore with everybody rowing, let alone when a guy stands up and starts putting his life jacket on.

—LOU HOLTZ

Tomorrow should be interesting, Andy thought. And that was just one of the hundred or so thoughts that were humming through his mind as he came out of the door and drifted across the parking lot. He didn't see the small car coming his way, and nearly jumped out of his skin as the driver slammed on the brakes and honked the horn, missing Andy by inches.

Heart pounding, Andy took a few deep breaths, tried to compose himself as best he could, and looked through the windshield at the driver. He recognized her immediately.

"Mariko?" he asked, stepping around from the front of the car to approach the driver's side.

"Andy-san!" she cried, rolling down the window. "You were almost a pancake!"

Mariko Tanaka Simpson was Scotty's martial arts instructor, and doubled as Lizzy's yoga instructor. Mariko owned the only martial arts and yoga

18

studio in town, which she had opened a few years back, shortly after coming to Twin Falls. She called it simply The Dojo, which in Japanese meant "place of the way," and in the martial arts world was used to denote the central gathering place for learning and training. Mariko was a *sensei*, or master, of a number of disciplines—*kung fu, aikido, jujitsu, win chun*—as she had grown up at the feet of her grand champion father. She taught her own unique blend of favorite techniques drawn from each discipline, but because she liked it that the word meant "way of balanced life energy," she called the method simply aikido. Most of her martial arts students were children and teenagers, but her yoga classes were popular among the adults. Like the Harmons, Mariko had moved to Twin Falls from Chicago, and at just around the same time, but for slightly different reasons. She was married to Axel Simpson, the service manager of Mainstreet Motors. Everyone called him Ax.

Mariko was tiny, barely over five feet tall, but she was a fierce competitor gifted with unrelenting tenacity and blazing speed. Andy had seen her in action during her periodic demonstrations at The Dojo, easily dispatching opponents twice her size using movements that Andy could barely see. She used the force and energy of her attackers— exploiting it, redirecting it, bending and blending it with her own to her advantage, safely and without any injury to her opponent.

"Sorry, I wasn't paying attention," said Andy. "Got a lot of stuff on my mind."

"Car trouble?" asked Mariko. "Ax will fix it."

"Trouble, yes," replied Andy. "Car trouble, no. A bit worse, I'm afraid."

He hesitated a moment, deciding whether this was the time and place to go into detail. But the Mega Box move might affect Mariko somewhat as well, since some of her students were from Mega Box families.

"Mega Box is moving. Everyone is unemployed, as of today. It's a terrible situation."

Mariko was quiet and solemn for a moment, taking in the news and noting how dejected Andy appeared. Then she brightened a bit, sat forward, and leaned out of the window. "*Kiki*," she grinned.

"It's not funny," replied Andy, frowning, a bit annoyed.

"No, no, Andy-san," Mariko corrected. "Not hee-hee, kiki. It means *crisis* in Japanese."

"Sorry. Then why the smile?" Andy asked.

Mariko quickly explained.

"The characters used to write kiki have two sets. One set means *danger*. The other set means *opportunity*. My father taught me to think about it like a rainstorm. After the thunder and lightning and rain, everything is fresh, green, renewed, and there is growth."

"Ah," replied Andy.

"You see only the danger now. It is visible and easy to see. You can feel it. It is harder to see the opportunity." Mariko paused a moment. "*Do* you see it yet, Andy-san?"

"To be honest with you, no," Andy answered.

"Hmm. Why are you here?" asked Mariko.

"Well," Andy hesitated, wondering how much to say. But he realized there was no point in keeping it a secret. "I asked Grady Carver for a job as salesman. I guess you could call it a job. Desk, chair, phone. No salary, all commission. He'll train me, though. It's something, anyway. Lizzy and the kids don't know I lost my job yet."

The corner of Mariko's mouth curled slightly. She waited, saying nothing, nodding. She gave it a moment, just watching and waiting. Andy was silent, biting his lip, not knowing what to say or do next. Mariko was patient. She felt sure Andy would realize what he had just described.

Suddenly Andy's eyes widened as the recognition dawned on him. "I get it," he said, nodding. "The closing has an upside. This may be it. I get it, I get your meaning. My father once told me the same sort of thing, make things happen, don't just let them. I get it!"

"Kiki!" repeated Mariko.

"Kiki it is," Andy agreed.

Mariko started her car and put her seatbelt around her once more, pleased and satisfied that Andy understood. "The most important thing is that you took a step, Andy-san. The storm will pass and things will grow." She put her car in gear, then stopped and put it back in neutral. "Later, you bring Scotty to class, okay? I have something to give you. Don't forget."

"Uh, sure," Andy said with a puzzled grin, asking, "What is it, some special yoga meditation thing to give me strength?"

"No, no. That's silly. You'll see. Don't forget." Mariko drove away, heading for the service drive to have lunch with Ax.

Andy stood in the parking lot, scratching his head as he watched her go. *Go figure. Parking lot wisdom. Kiki. Danger and opportunity, two sides of the same coin. Good thought. I like that. But what in the world is she going to give me?*

Andy got in his car feeling better than he had all day, which wasn't saying all that much. But on the drive home he started to relax, mulling over the Mainstreet Motors meeting, and his new so-called job. *That was easy. Maybe too easy. There goes Saturday with the kids. It's not ideal, but I've gotta make this work. We've got some money put away, we'll be fine. But not forever. I've got to make this work. I can sell. Can I sell cars? How hard can it be? What's Lizzy going to think? She'll be happy just knowing we're staying put, right?*

As he pulled into his driveway for the second time that day, he noticed that everyone was home from school. It wasn't even four o'clock, and he knew they'd all want to know why he was home so early.

He walked through the front door and into the kitchen, where the after-school snack roundup was in high gear. Lizzy, Scotty, and Sandra all stopped what they were doing and looked at him.

"Daddy!" chorused the kids, racing over to give him a hug. "You're home!"

"Honey?" inquired Lizzy, tentatively.

Andy sat down at the table and said in a quiet voice: "Hi, guys. Listen, I've got some good news, and some bad news."

Challenges make you discover things about yourself that you never really knew. They're what make the instrument stretch, they're what make you go beyond the norm.

—CICELY TYSON

the preparation

He who every morning plans the transactions of the day, and follows
out the plan, carries on a thread which will guide him through the
labyrinth of the most busy life.

The orderly arrangement of his time is like a ray of light which darts itself
through all his affairs. But where no plan is laid, where the disposal
of time is surrendered merely to the chance of incidents,
all things lie huddled together in one chaos.

−HUGH BLAIR

To Andy's surprise, the Harmon family took the
news in stride. Lizzy was nothing but supportive.
"No matter what happens, we'll find a way," she
said. Sandra, being too young to fully understand,
was just glad that daddy was home early.

Scotty was the most excited. To him, cars of
any kind were very cool. Business and managing a
call center hadn't meant much to him when Andy
had explained his job at Mega Box. But he could
really relate to his dad's work now, and he raced
out of the house to tell his friends that his dad was

going to be selling cars. Not fifteen minutes later, he bolted back through the front door, explaining between gasps that it was time to go to The Dojo.

"It's Kaizen Night!" Scotty cried. "Everybody has to come!"

"You're right," Lizzy nodded. "I forgot that tonight is another one, but it's on the calendar. Third Friday of every month."

"Kaizen Night?" Andy asked. He wasn't familiar with it. *How did I not know about this? Seems like a big thing to Scotty.*

"You'll see," Scotty said, nodding and grabbing Andy's hand to lead him out to the car. "You always were at work before. Now you can come. Let's go."

On the way to The Dojo, Andy told Lizzy about his meeting Mariko in the Mainstreet Motors lot. He told her about the lesson of kiki, and that Mariko had something for him.

"Now I'm curious," Lizzy said. "I love her Zen perspective on things. I always learn something from these Kaizen Nights. Mariko talks about things in the context of aikido and martial arts, but if you listen close and think about her message, what she says can be applied to any part of life."

"What do you mean?" Andy asked.

"Well, take the kiki thing," Lizzy answered. "Mariko says much of the reason the Chinese developed martial arts in the first place all those thousands of years ago was to turn a disadvantage into an advantage, and a potentially dangerous situation into a safe one."

"Thousands?" Andy asked.

"Oh yes," Lizzy confirmed. "When Scotty first started I did some reading at the library during my breaks. Some say as far back as four thousand years. It started out as a means of military combat. But over the centuries it was adopted by non-military—farmers, priests—as a means of self-defense, mostly without weapons. It grew as Chinese society did, merged with the evolution of Buddhism in Zen Buddhism, spread to other parts of Asia, and over time came to center on a philosophy that seeks to cultivate a person's physical, mental, and spiritual energies. So it's not just about self-defense, and my yoga isn't just about stretching. A key element to both is mindfulness. That's the Zen part. It's why I meditate the way Mariko taught me."

"Ohmmmm," Andy said piously, casting his eyes down.

"Too touchy-feely for ya, big guy?" Lizzy chided.

"Nah," Andy answered, shaking his head. "It makes sense. It's a whole system."

"Sure, Mr. All-Business-All-the-Time," Lizzy said, giving Andy a playful slap on the arm. "If you want to think about it like that. I prefer the softer, gentler blending of hands, head, and heart myself."

"Well, obviously there's something to it all with that kind of staying power," Andy concluded.

"I'd say," Lizzy nodded. "Aikido is one of the newest variants, but it's still almost a hundred years old."

"Here we are," Andy announced, pulling in to the small parking lot.

They entered The Dojo just in time to hear Mariko's introduction.

"Welcome everyone to Kaizen Night. Most of you know me, but I see a few new faces here tonight, so please allow me to introduce both myself and tonight's activities. I am Mariko, sensei of The Dojo. On the third Friday of each month, we invite everyone to Kaizen Night. Tonight the students will perform for you the basic forms that they have been practicing. A basic form is a foundational regimen, which we call a *kata*.

"A kata is a standardized set of movements that the student must learn and master so that it becomes a natural pattern of behavior that is as fluid as walking or breathing or riding a bicycle. When these movements become automatic, we need not think about them. They become an extension of ourselves and of our behavior. When they become second nature, we can act reflexively, creatively, improvising as needed and focusing not on technique but on the strategy, the opposing forces, and our own performance.

"As most of you know, I require my students to master a simple kata before progressing to a more advanced one. For example, a kata with twenty-seven moves must be mastered before attempting one with fifty-four moves, which in turn must be mastered before attempting one with a hundred and eight moves. Twice a year students may take a test that covers several katas, and this allows them to advance the degree and color of their belt.

"But tonight is not about a test or the achievement of a specific level of aptitude. It is simply to allow the students to demonstrate their progress over the past month. This demonstration before an audience helps the pattern of movements become more automatic, more quickly, because the students must focus so much more intently. Kaizen Night is also a recognition of the incremental progress the students have made, for that is part of the *kaizen* philosophy.

"Kaizen in Japanese loosely translates to 'continuous improvement.' The characters of the word are in two sets. The first, *kai*, means 'change.' The second set, *zen*, means 'better.' Change for the better. I was taught that kaizen is at once a philosophy, a principle, and a practice. It is used by individuals, teams, and business organizations in many different spheres of activity to continuously improve and get better. I believe it to be a true path to mastery and lasting change.

"Kaizen as a philosophy recognizes that perfection should be treated not as a goal to be achieved but rather as an aim and a never-ending pursuit, because there is no limit on better. In fact, the kaizen philosophy rests on the belief that there is no best, only better. As a principle, kaizen holds that taking small and steady steps, rather than large and rapid leaps, is the key to confidently and constantly moving forward, and thus achieving long-term success.

"As a practice, or perhaps as a process, kaizen has three essential steps: create a standard, follow it, and search for a better way. A kata can be thought of as that standard. It is the starting point of the journey.

"I must tell you that if you were here last month, you may not be able to see the improvement that has been made by your child. Do not worry, for I can. Take comfort in knowing that if you did not attend another Kaizen Night for six months, upon your return you would easily see the change. In fact, you would be amazed to see how much, and how well, your child has improved.

> When you improve a little bit each day, eventually big things occur. Don't look for big, quick improvement. Instead, seek small improvement one day at a time. That's the only way it happens—and when it happens, it lasts.
>
> —JOHN WOODEN

"That is because above all else, kaizen is about how to achieve big leaps through small steps."

Andy listened intently, absorbing Mariko's words. Amazed, he watched Scotty perform his kata energetically, with surprising precision. Andy could only admire Scotty's focus and determination. The children received a standing ovation from all of the proud parents in the audience.

"Thank you all for coming tonight," Mariko announced after the children had performed. "I hope you enjoyed this evening. It means a lot to the class that you are here. I know that today was one of challenge for many people in Twin Falls. I wish you all good fortune."

With that, Mariko gave a quick bow.

Andy approached her, with Lizzy and Sandra in tow. "Tonight was amazing."

"Thank you! The kids were so great, don't you think? So glad you came," Mariko said, giving another little bow. "Wait right here. I have something to give you."

They watched as Mariko retreated to a small storeroom closet located just outside the small office. They heard a muffled but triumphant "aha!" and Mariko returned with a strange-looking figurine that had no arms or legs. It was an oddly shaped, bottom-heavy, roly-poly face, with a fierce scowl and daunting black beard. The whites of the eyes were blank, with no pupils. Surrounding the face was a red ceremonial hood with gold trim.

"This is for you," Mariko said, offering the doll to Andy with both hands. Everyone jumped a bit when a voice cried, "What is that?" Scotty had quietly come up behind them, joining the family.

"This is a Daruma doll," Mariko replied, retrieving the doll from Andy and kneeling to place it on the floor. "You see?" she asked, tumbling the doll over. "How it regains its balance? It symbolizes an undaunted spirit and recovery from misfortune."

Scotty nodded, eyes wide.

Mariko continued her story. "Daruma is the nickname, you might say, of Bodhidharma, a Buddhist monk who lived in the fifth century. It was he who founded Zen Buddhism. He's the father of Zen, in a way. As the legend goes, Daruma-san lost the use of his arms and legs after sitting motionless for eight years in a cave, engaged in meditation, seeking enlightenment. He was successful. Daruma achieved the ultimate balance. The doll in his likeness is now a symbol of good luck and protection in Japan."

"But why are the eyes blank?" Andy asked.

"Ah," replied Mariko. "It is tradition to give a Daruma doll to one who is starting out on a new venture, taking a new direction, or making a transition. At the start of the endeavor, one makes a wish

and paints in one eye, usually the doll's left. The other eye is painted when the goal is successfully attained."

Andy accepted the Daruma doll graciously, repeating his gratitude. "Thank you, Mariko, I appreciate your thoughtfulness. I need all the luck I can get."

The Daruma doll was a nice gesture, thought Andy. *Unusual, but nice.*

34

At dinner, Andy was noticeably distracted and quiet. The kids thought the Daruma doll was cool and took turns at dinner trying to topple it, finally leaving it to rest in the middle of the table as a sort of centerpiece. Lizzy sensed Andy's preoccupation and made sure that she and the kids went on as if nothing out of the ordinary had happened that day. She focused the discussion on Kaizen Night.

"You know, there's some science to what Mariko told us about kaizen," she began. "There's a part of our brains that doesn't handle change very well. It's called the amygdala."

"Sounds like Godzilla," Scotty quipped.

"Godzilla brain!" Sandra giggled.

"Hush," Lizzy continued. "The amygdala is hard-wired to protect us. It controls what's known as the fight-or-flight response. That's what has helped humans survive and evolve. When there's danger, it sends an alarm signal to shut down anything that might block our ability to fight a threat or run away from it. That means it shuts down the other parts of the brain, like the one that governs thinking and creativity."

That piqued Andy's curiosity. "Say more. What's that have to do with kaizen?"

"Well, there's a little problem with that wiring," Lizzy continued. "Any time there's any kind of change from the usual, those alarm bells go off. Anything out of the ordinary registers as danger, and fear kicks in. The bigger the change, the bigger the fear factor. We can't help it. The smaller the change, the smaller the fear."

"Okay, so . . ." Andy prompted.

"So," Lizzy concluded, "Since kaizen is about smaller and safer steps—small change—we don't shut off the thinking and creating part as much. It tricks the brain enough to move forward in a positive way with focus and purpose—not just run or freeze up or fight senselessly."

Andy took it all in, thankful for Lizzy's science background. *I suppose things happen and come together for a reason*, he conceded.

After dinner, Andy took the Daruma doll off the table and assigned it a spot on the top shelf in his den without giving it any further thought.

The next morning found Andy sitting in his car parked in the employee lot of Mainstreet Motors, thirty minutes before he had to be there. He hadn't slept much. As he reflected on the day before, he couldn't help but think how odd it had been. In fact, it had been one of the most unusual in his life, and the shock to his system made him realize how much of a routine he had been in.

It felt strange to be away from home on a Saturday, almost wrong. He was sacrificing one of the most important things of all: time on the weekends with his family. He had promised to come home at lunchtime. As he waited in the car for someone to show up, he glanced through the Saturday edition of the *Sentinel*. Sure enough, the story of the Mega Box departure had been hastily constructed at the last hour. The Sunday edition would surely run a full feature, and Andy half expected a reporter to call him for comment.

He had already started mapping out his plan of attack. He knew he needed to get to know the dealership's way of doing business. He knew he needed to learn about the products and services he would be selling. He knew he needed a plan.

A rap on the window jolted him out of his thoughts. Grady Carver. Smiling as always. Andy got out of his car and greeted Grady.

"Well?" Grady said, smiling even wider, "Ready for this?"

"As I'll ever be," replied Andy, demonstrating as much enthusiasm as he could.

"Good! Today's our busiest day, and tomorrow is second, so your job is to watch what goes on. Shadow the guys, see how they do deals. I'll have you sit with me in the tower later in the day. Watch how they do things differently for new versus used cars. The focus is new, remember that. New cars cost me money every minute they sit on the floor. The used ones I've already sunk the cost. Sit in the Finance office, get to know the paperwork. Things get slow, grab the manuals and start learning the models. Features, advantages, benefits, it's all there in black and white. Come Monday, you can drive the demos to get a feel. End of next week, I'll have you try a walkaround sales presentation . . . you can try to sell me a car as you walk around it. I figure you're ready in about ten days to do a deal, start to close. That's the standard ramp-up. Don't worry, I'm there to slam-dunk the deal if you get in trouble."

It was a lot to take in for Andy. This would take some getting used to. *Ten days!* He definitely needed a plan for making that time work to his advantage. He could not leave things to chance or circumstance.

As the morning progressed, the cold reality of Andy's situation finally began to sink in.

What did I get myself into? he thought.

The whole approach to business was different from what he was accustomed to. The sales team wasn't really a team as much as it was a bunch of guys with the same goal and title competing for the same business under one roof. There was a winner-take-all feeling, and it seemed to Andy that the customer was on the losing end of the game. *Can I even work in this kind of system?*

Andy was so deep in thought he didn't realize that someone had walked up and was standing next to him. Axel Simpson.

"So what do you think so far?" asked Axel, as if he were reading Andy's mind. "Crazy, huh?"

"Axel, hi!" Andy cried. "I didn't even see you there. Yep, different for sure."

"Call me Ax. I hear yesterday was pretty different too. Kiki, kaizen, kata. All the K's, all at once. Lucky you. Head spinning?"

"You could say that. It's been a whirlwind twenty-four hours, to say the least," Andy agreed. "I'm just trying to stay afloat, take it all in, make sense of things. Not even sure that's possible. On the other hand, all these new ideas somehow hang together in a way. The timing must be good. Does that sound weird?"

"Not to me," said Ax. "But then I'm married to Mariko. And I hear she gave you a Daruma doll, huh? She gave me one when I set my sights on one day making service manager."

"I haven't done it yet," said Andy. "Color in an eye, I mean."

"You sorta need to set your sights on something first," replied Ax. "No pun intended."

"Not sure I have a specific goal in mind," said Andy. "Other than regaining my balance. Kind of like the doll does, I guess."

> Our plans miscarry because they have no aim. When a man does not know what harbor he is making for, no wind is the right wind.
>
> —MARCUS ANNAEUS SENECA

"It doesn't need to be exact," said Ax. "Regaining lost balance works fine. It's your journey, and

40

you just need to maybe figure out what that'll look like when you get there. Doing your *hoshin* helps."

Andy cocked his head at the new term. "Hoshin?"

"Hoshin," confirmed Axel. "*Hoshin kanri* is the full phrase. Mariko taught it to me, and I use it personally and here at work too. Hoshin means aim, or direction, or even plan. Kanri means, administration or management, or even control. In Japanese it suggests the shining of a metal compass needle, the one leading all the individual units of the group toward the goal. So in business, it's really about setting a strategic direction, then setting a course of action that is deployed throughout the organization. Lower goals, interim goals, all have to align. Then vision becomes reality. It's helped the Service team. We have a goal of 100 percent 'fixed right, first time.' It's our core score that keeps us focused, helps align all our processes. We've got short-term goals supporting the long-term goal. The rest of the store doesn't get the hoshin thing."

"Well, I get it," said Andy. "And I like it. I know I need a plan."

"Here's the visual," said Axel. "Geese flying in the V formation. Individuals all, but all heading in the same direction, all aligned."

"Got it," nodded Andy.

"Listen," said Axel, "I know you need to get to work. Not to dump more Japanese terms on you, but Mariko calls it *genchi genbutsu*. Means 'go look, go see.' You have to do that before you can do your hoshin, because it allows you to grasp the situation and fully understand what's going on. Observation is the key. Observe first, plan second."

"Gen-chee, what?" Andy repeated, slowly.

"It's gen-chee gen-boot-soo," Axel chuckled. "Since you're in the car biz now, you should know that a famous automotive manufacturing engineer named Taiichi Ohno used to teach new workers how to do genchi genbutsu by telling them to draw a circle on the floor in front of an operation. He'd say, 'stand in the circle and watch the process and think for yourself.' No hint of what to watch for. He'd say, 'Just keep asking why?' Sometimes they'd be in the circle all day."

"So what happened after all that time?" asked Andy.

"What happened was they got familiar with the process in a hurry!" said Axel. "And then they'd start to see problems, gaps, opportunities for improvement. They'd tell Ohno what they thought, and he would just look at them and say, 'Is that so?' He was teaching them to think."

"Why do I feel like I'm in an episode of that old TV show *Kung Fu* all of a sudden?" Andy asked ruefully. "And I'm the grasshopper."

"Maybe a little *Karate Kid* thrown in too . . . wax-on, wax-off!" Axel said with a laugh. "Just take it slow, one step at a time. Kaizen, my man. Big goal, small steps. Gotta run!"

Axel gave a wave over his head as he beat a path back to the Service Department.

Andy watched him go. He had the same feeling as the day before, after Mariko's lesson in kiki.

At the end of the day, Grady Carver approached Andy to check in and check up. "Listen, you look dazed and confused. Sorry I didn't get a chance to touch base earlier. Today was a pretty good day, not great, but everyone sold at least one, mostly new, coupla used. Next week is the big end-of-the-month tent sale. We've got big incentives

43

on almost every new car, and I want you to be ready enough to pitch in. I think you have a feel for what goes on here, and you probably need some time to digest it all. I'm not here tomorrow anyway, so take it off, spend some time with the product manuals. I'll see you Monday, same time, same channel."

"Thanks, Grady," answered Andy. "Not necessary, but I appreciate it. I could use the time to start planning things out."

Grady shot Andy a quizzical look, like *Plan? what on earth are you talking about?* but said nothing, turned and waved as he retreated.

Andy was exhausted by the time he arrived home at seven that evening. The day was even more of a blur than yesterday had been, if that was possible. He hadn't made it home at lunchtime, there simply wasn't time. He had watched all the goings-on, but it only confused him. The sales team had been too busy trying to sell cars to explain anything. Not that it would have helped . . . everyone seemed to be speaking their own special language. If there was a consistent process or anything even remotely resembling a kata, he couldn't see it. New cars were sold differently from used ones, and the whole trade-in transaction was a complete mystery, as was the wide variety in schemes and approaches to price negotiation. One word described the entire experience: pressure. As he thought about Grady Carver's intent for him to sell a car next week, Andy felt the weight of his decision.

As he walked through the front door, he saw that things were winding down, and that he had missed dinner for the first time in a long time.

"Are you okay?" asked Lizzy worriedly. "How did it go? We missed you today."

"I'm not sure about this whole thing," replied Andy. "It's different, that's for sure. But the good news is I'm here all day tomorrow. Let's go do something fun. I'm exhausted. I need a break."

Monday morning came a bit too early for Andy, as he stood in front of the mirror knotting his tie. Sunday had been the perfect remedy. He and Lizzy had taken the kids on a long picnic hike, out and away from everything on a weather-perfect day. Andy had forgotten most of his troubles, and everything about his new job, deciding to put his energy into his personal life and postponing any thoughts of work. But now it was time to turn his attention to professional concerns.

As he was packing up his briefcase in the den, Andy's eyes drifted upward, settling on the Daruma doll, still perched where he had set it Friday night.

Why not? he thought, grabbing the Daruma doll and marching out to the garage. There he found some old black enamel and a small brush he and Scotty had used to paint a model Corvette a few months back. Carefully, and with as steady a hand as he could muster, Andy painted in the left eye and set the Daruma doll down on the workbench to dry. *The other one is to be filled in when everything is back to normal around here,* he thought, rinsing the brush in paint thinner and setting it aside to dry. *Balance regained. We'll have that in common, Mr. Daruma doll.*

Driving in to Mainstreet Motors, he began to think through the coming week.

There's only one way to do this, he thought. *Jump in full force, learn everything I can as fast as I can to get my bearings, then set my course and build my plan. Genchi genbutsu, hoshin kanri. Genchi genbutsu, hoshin kanri.*

By lunchtime on Wednesday, Andy knew his way around the dealership, and around a vehicle. He made an effort to meet everyone working at the store. Then he methodically made his way through every facet of the operation. He spent time with the porters, learning how to detail a car. He watched custom-ers come and go, a few buying, most leaving. He watched cars being delivered. He listened to customer service calls. He watched how service advisers handled customers who'd come in to get their cars repaired and maintained. He drove every model Mainstreet sold, at least once. He watched the sales consultants. He saw how financing and insurance was handled. He wasn't ready to sell a car yet, or even role-play with Grady Carver. But he was ready to start planning for how he would build his business.

> It is when things go hardest, when life becomes most trying, that there is greatest need for having a fixed goal. When few comforts come from without, it is all the more necessary to have a fount to draw on from within.
>
> —B. C. FORBES

Grady Carver had set a time for their walkaround role-play presentation for Friday afternoon, four o'clock. Andy decided that he would present his sales plan to Grady at that time.

Thursday night, after the kids were asleep and Lizzy was immersed in her latest historical novel, Andy sat down at the kitchen table and began mapping out his strategy. His hoshin.

At the top of the page, he listed what he considered his personal strengths and assets that he should exploit, as well as opportunities he could pursue. Andy knew he had three things going for him—relationship-building skill, outside sales experience from his career in Chicago, and customer service phone experience from Mega Box.

Now he needed to figure out a way to put those elements to use in his new capacity as an automobile salesman.

He had noticed that the sales consultants in the dealership were completely reactive in their approach to business, which was understandable for a retail store. Still, they basically stood in an informal line awaiting their turn at bat. In fact, they referred to shoppers as "ups."

There's a better way, thought Andy. *Not a huge change. But better. Kaizen.*

The seeds of a different approach began to take root in his brain. Within the hour, Andy had the makings of what he thought was a pretty good plan:

Strategic Goals
1. Know features, advantages, and benefits of all models and trims.
2. Know demographics and psychographics of all customer segments.
3. Construct target list of "warm prospects" from personal network.
4. Construct target list of "warm prospects" from dealership database of customers in third, fourth, and fifth year of ownership.
5. Construct target list of "warm prospects" from dealership database of customers with repetitive service problems.
6. Use proactive approach to build business, via phone and appointment setting.
7. Use proactive approach to build business, via target mailings.
8. Use proactive approach to build business, via social gatherings and trade association membership.

9. Treat unsolicited showroom visitors as second-ary source of business.
10. Take the long-term view: build customer relation-ships rather than holding a sell-today mentality.

Objectives:
- One unit/week within thirty days
- Two units/week within sixty days
- Three units/week within ninety days

If I start off with thirty calls a day, I should be able to set at least seven appointments a week, thought Andy. *If I sell half that number, I'm on track.*

Andy was satisfied with his plan. It would be hard work, he knew, but the approach was different from what was happening in the store now. The strategy made best use of his skills and experience, and it made sense. He was pretty sure no one else had such a plan. Grady Carver should be pleasantly surprised. In any event, he'd present it to him tomorrow.

By the time Friday afternoon rolled around, Andy was ready to demonstrate his week of learning and prep. Grady Carver gathered the entire team for Andy's walkaround of a brand new one-ton pickup truck. Andy hadn't been expecting an audience, but he was comfortable enough to go on as planned. The whole thing brought back the memory of Kaizen Night, and it occurred to Andy that he was giving his version of a kata.

"Not bad!" praised Grady, after Andy had spent twenty minutes going through his routine, showing and telling. "A few minor glitches, but not bad at all. Take a lesson, gentlemen," he said, ribbing the rest. "There's a new kid on the block."

> In the space of two days I had evolved two plans, wholly distinct, both of which were equally feasible. The point I am trying to bring out is that one does not plan and then try to make circumstances fit those plans. One tries to make plans fit the circumstances.
>
> —GEORGE PATTON

Grady turned back to Andy, "Whaddaya say, wanna give it a shot tomorrow?"

"Sure," answered Andy. Truth be told, he would have liked another week to prepare. He wasn't at all confident that he had truly mastered his routine, his kata.

"Good!" smiled Grady.

As the group dispersed, Andy caught up to Grady. "Got a minute, Grady? I want to show you what I've come up with as far as a game plan goes."

"Game plan?" asked Grady, somewhat distracted. "What game plan? Customer comes in, you sell. You sell, sell, sell. Hit the nut, that's the plan. You get better as you go. What else is there?"

"It just seems like a big waste waiting around for people to come in the door," urged Andy. "I came up with something that might work better, at least for me."

"Hey, no offense, Andy, but I don't care what you do to make the number. I don't need to see the theory. We've got metal to move. You do whatever it takes. I'll help you this next week in closing the deals, then you're on your own."

And with that, Grady Carver walked away, saying over his shoulder, "See you tomorrow. And Sunday's your day off until further notice."

Slightly stunned, Andy packed up and headed home.

Strange management style, he thought. *Oh well, tomorrow marks day one of putting the plan in place. I'm a bit ahead of schedule, but that's okay.*

As he pulled into the garage that night, he saw the Daruma doll on the work-bench, where he had left it Monday morning.

> As I look back upon my life, I see that every part of it was a preparation for the next. The most trivial of incidents fits into the larger pattern like a mosaic in a preconceived design.
>
> —MARGARET SANGER

Collecting the doll and returning it to the top shelf in his den, he thought:

Let's go, my one-eyed friend.

the struggle

If there is no struggle there is no progress. Those who profess to favor freedom and yet deprecate agitation, are men who want crops without plowing up the ground, they want rain without thunder and lightning. They want the ocean without the awful roar of its many waters. This struggle may be a moral one, or it may be a physical one, and it may be both moral and physical, but it must be a struggle.

—FREDERICK DOUGLASS

Andy wasn't even able to think about his plan when Saturday came. It was perhaps the longest and most difficult day of his professional life. It wasn't so much that he didn't sell a car, because he didn't expect to. It had to do with the process. It was, in a word, painful. And it sent a clear signal to Andy that the road ahead of him would be a lot rougher than he had anticipated.

The day had begun as usual, the major difference being that today, Andy was no longer in observation mode. Today, he went live. He knew that Saturday was the busiest day of the week. To make matters worse, the weekend tent sale marked the month's close, which meant the monthly objective had to be hit. With drastic price cuts and big incentives, the store was nothing short of chaotic. Radio commercials and newspaper ads had resulted in a wave of customers looking for a deal. The sales team was in overdrive. Even the Service Department was open.

Andy needed help, but no one was available to lend a much-needed hand. Grady Carver would have been the most likely prospect, but not only was he swamped with transactions, Andy never even got to the point where he had a real buyer. The most shocking thing to Andy was the adversarial nature of the interaction. His very first attempt threw him off-kilter for the remainder of the day.

When the doors opened at eight, it was all hands on deck to cope with the shoppers. Andy had the immediate opportunity to introduce himself to a young couple with a small child. As he approached them, the husband immediately offered a terse: "We're just looking."

"Not a problem," answered Andy. "If you have questions, just let me know. If I don't have the answers, I'll find someone who does. There's a small play area for kids over there, by the way."

"He'll be fine with us, thanks," answered the husband.

As Andy turned to walk toward other shoppers, the husband stopped him. "What do you know about this one?" he demanded.

To Andy, that was the opportunity to start a dialogue. Andy's instincts were to find out about the family, what their needs were, why they were looking for a new car, and a host of other things that would help him help them to find the best fit. But they weren't having any of it, and try as he might, the husband kept pointing to the model, saying, "I just want to know about this one."

As Andy prepared to launch into what he thought was his first product presentation, he was interrupted repeatedly. "What other colors are there? Is this price in the paper real? How's this compare with the other brand's competing model? I know these mileage figures are inflated; what's the real number? I know the invoice on this car, why's the sticker so high?"

It seemed to Andy that he was doing battle rather than trying to help someone make an informed decision. For over an hour, he answered the questions as best he could. He showed what he could of the car. He asked what questions he could, as best he could. He tried to get to know the couple and their child. But to no avail. There would be no rapport built with these people. In the end, the couple left without wanting a card, without a handshake. An abrupt "Thanks, we'll keep looking" was about all Andy got in the way of feedback.

As he looked around the showroom, three of the sales consultants already had buyers in their office penciling deals, one was out on a test drive, and one was enthusiastically conducting a walka-round. He shot Andy a smirk.

That was rough. I'm not ready, he thought. *I don't know my kata well enough, obviously. I didn't even use it. I failed the first test. Dismal.*

"Round one goes to the shopper," a voice said behind him, startling him. It was Axel Simpson. "Breathe."

"Ax, hey," sighed Andy. "Yeah, by a knockout, I'd say."

"Don't look so glum," Axel urged. "Listen, you're so new at this it would be a miracle if you made a sale on your first go. It's going to take awhile."

"I know, but still," replied Andy. "I didn't do anything right."

"Not true," said Axel. "I saw a little. You did better than you think. You're not in The Dojo rehearsing your kata without an opponent. This is the real deal. You're doing battle. There's pushback. You're doing fine."

> Virtually nothing comes out right the first time. Failures, repeated failures, are finger posts on the road to achievement. The only time you don't want to fail is the last time you try something. One fails forward toward success.
>
> —CHARLES F. KETTERING

"Well, thanks," smiled Andy. "Can I buy you a cup of coffee? I need a little boost."

"That's where I was headed when your sparring match caught my eye," nodded Axel.

They ordered coffee from the little showroom snack nook and sat at a small table.

"You know," began Axel, "Mariko told me that the first time she ever competed she got trounced. Didn't get a single point. Her opponent had a countermove for everything—had a lot more experience. She was at the same developmental level, but he had seen more competitive matches, more variations. Listen, nobody wins first time out.

Everyone knows that. You're supposed to get beat up a little. It's part of the process."

"I know, I know," Andy nodded. "Man, it's just hard starting over at the beginning. I'm a rank amateur. In this arena, anyway. But I remember my first sales job in Chicago. Outside sales, pharmaceuticals. Didn't make a sale on my first call. In fact, I just about got thrown out of the doctor's office. Crotchety old curmudgeon type . . . had no use for me or what I had to offer. So you're right."

"So go easy on yourself," said Axel. "You gotta learn by failing a little. Improve as you go. It's the kaizen way, and you'll get better. Just make sure you don't forget your *hansei*. It's an important part of kaizen."

"Hahn-say," said Andy, repeating the sounds slowly. "I'll add it to my growing glossary. What is it, what's it mean?"

"It means *reflection*," replied Axel, "but its closer meaning is *introspection*. Its roots are in Zen philosophy and religion, but it is a profound skill to be mastered. Japanese schoolchildren are taught from kindergarten how to perform hansei, and it's a must-do in order to learn and improve."

"Children learn it?"

"Absolutely," replied Axel. "They're taught to do it regularly, as a discipline, without thinking about results."

"Not sure I follow." Andy was shaking his head.

"Well," continued Axel, "in other words, it doesn't matter if you got an A or a C on your report card, you conduct hansei in both cases to better understand the process that led to the specific result. But . . ."

"But?" asked Andy.

"But here's the thing," said Axel, knitting his brows. "It's a discipline we here in the West don't much value . . . the process of unwrapping things, every time, irrespective of the outcome. Mostly we do a postmortem when we fail at something, but too often the goal is fault-finding and blame, not real learning. And mostly we high-five and pop champagne if we exceed all expectations, and leave it with a big attaboy. For example, if you come home with a D in math you're scolded and told to work harder. Maybe there's some discussion of the trouble areas, but not much. Come with an A in math, Mom and Dad reward you. And there's no debrief at all, because after all, you got an A."

"So what's wrong with that?" asked Andy. "Seems normal to me."

"Trouble is," explained Axel, "there's no real learning in that whole approach. But whether you miss a mark under or over, there's a gap there that demands better understanding. *If* we want to get better, that is."

"I never thought of it that way," Andy nodded. "So what's the hansei process?"

"It's pretty simple," replied Axel. "Which raises the question of why we don't do it more often, or regularly. Have you ever heard of an after-action review?"

"Nope," said Andy.

"The U.S. Army developed it, and it's the practical way to perform hansei. They use it to build practical on-the-job learning into every activity—doesn't matter if you're taking inventory at a base kitchen or facing enemy fire. It's so much a part of what they do it's now a verb. Got some buddies in the forces, and they'll be telling me about some deployment, and they'll say 'then we AARed it.' And it's dirt simple to do."

"I'm listening," said Andy, relieved to have a practical to-do item. "I like dirt simple."

"It's three questions," stated Axel. "What was supposed to happen? What actually happened? Why are there differences? If there are any, that is."

"So let me get this right," began Andy. "In the case of the school kid with an A, you ask those three questions. Maybe the answer to the first question is B. The answer to the second is A. So there's a gap, a difference. And knowing what caused the gap helps you learn how to do things better in the future."

"Yep," nodded Axel. "And, the fruit of a good hansei is a new and revised hoshin. You can better set and adjust your interim targets. Hansei is performed regularly, after every action. So the school kid does it for every quiz, test, paper, you name it, not just the end grade. In business, if you have a ten-phase project, you do it after every key milestone."

"So you do it individually and as a group?" asked Andy.

"Yes," replied Axel. "My point here was you should AAR your interactions today with each customer purchase opportunity. But yes, we use it for formal hoshin purposes. We use the insights from our various hansei meetings to set new goals, strategies, directions. But there's some rules."

"Rules?" asked Andy.

"Sure," said Axel. "We make it safe to tell the absolute truth. That means we have to have rules. First, attendance by all involved is mandatory—no show, no AAR. No outside parties—if you weren't involved, you don't attend. No fault-finding or blaming—we focus on tasks and goals only. Specific facts are confidential and to be used for analysis, learning, and improvement only—no personnel actions arising from AARs allowed."

"Ax, this has been very helpful," said Andy. "I'm filing the group part for future reference, but I can do hansei starting now. Can't thank you enough."

"Sure. Oh, and get yourself one of these," Axel said, waving a slim black journal.

"What is that?" asked Andy.

"Performance journal," replied Axel matter-of-factly. "Got everything in here, and all my personal and professional hansei notes go in here."

"I'm not much of a writer," wavered Andy.

"It's not a diary of thoughts and feelings so much as it is a tracking device," Axel explained. "Basically it's a record of your hansei. But you treat it like any kata, right? It's a daily routine of recording all your key decisions and actions along with a projection of the expected outcome. Just like we talked about. You keep monitoring and reviewing your performance and satisfaction, feeding back from actual outcomes to expectations. Over time, trends and patterns show up that point out strengths and weaknesses."

"I'll pick one up ASAP," Andy said. "I gotta get back, but this is all good stuff. Again, thanks!"

"Get to it!" Axel smiled, pumping a fist.

By the end of the day, Andy had helped a total of four more customers. One was friendly enough, but turned out to be a car buff just wanting to talk about cars; he took up nearly three hours stringing Andy along, going through nearly every model in the lineup. Another listened sullenly as Andy presented the model, then left after refusing a demonstration drive. One stayed engaged through the demonstration drive, then left. The last one came in with a printout from the Internet and asked if Andy could match the price, leaving when Andy didn't immediately answer in the affirmative.

Each time, though, Andy got a little bit better, and he became just a bit more comfortable. He did a quick hansei after each experience. Every time he did, he found something he could improve upon and try on the next go-round. His kata evolved throughout the day. He tried hard not to be discouraged, but it was tough. *This whole kaizen thing might be simple, but it ain't easy. Not surprised the rest of the store doesn't do it. Huge effort required.*

By six o'clock, Andy was frazzled and ready to head for home. Grady Carver came over to Andy as he was preparing to leave.

"How'd your plan work out?" he asked, with a tone Andy found something less than sincere.

"Oh, well, today was so busy I didn't even have time for that," replied Andy. "Too many shoppers today."

"How'd you do?" asked Grady.

"Okay, I guess," answered Andy. "I'm still trying to figure things out."

"Yeah," said Grady. "Listen, about that. I watched you for a little while. Gotta tell ya, Andy, I didn't much like what I saw. Ya gotta put the pressure on more. Get 'em in your office. Corner 'em. Don't let 'em walk. Sell a dang car. Forget about making nice all the time. You have to try a lot harder. Push it, man, push it! Metal must be moved. I'd like you to come in tomorrow even though it's your day off. It's month end. If you sell something, anything, it helps."

"Okay," replied Andy. "I see what you're saying."

Andy watched Grady walk away. *That's not me. I can't come at people that way. I've got to work my plan. I'll stick it out for another day, then start making calls on Monday.*

Sunday didn't go much better for Andy, at least in terms of actually making a sale. The pressure was on to sell something, but he didn't. The store wasn't quite as busy as Saturday, but everyone sold at least one car except Andy. He tried to push more, but it only seemed to make things worse. Grady Carver didn't even look at him as he walked by on his way to his car at the end of the day.

Not a good sign, thought Andy, feeling the pressure.

Driving home, he was glad the weekend was over. He had gotten better, but he still felt disconnected from the Grady Carver way of conducting business. It was just too forced. Too unnatural. Tomorrow he could start putting his plan in place, doing things his way.

By Tuesday evening, Andy had yet to pick up the phone. Between studying the product book, building his database, and developing and rehearsing a special telephone kata, his time had been consumed. Everyone else in the store, though, had made a sale.

Grady Carver popped into Andy's office on his way out.

"Any reason why you've passed on your 'ups' last coupla days?" he asked. "Some aversion to making money I should know about?"

"Not at all," Andy said with a smile. "I'm just trying to get all my ducks in a row here."

> Whatever course you decide upon, there is always someone to tell you that you are wrong. There are always difficulties arising which tempt you to believe that your critics are right. To map out a course of action and follow it to an end requires courage.
>
> —RALPH WALDO EMERSON

"Get 'em lined up quick or your goose is cooked," Grady retorted. "Clock's ticking, don't forget. You're actually over the ten-day mark. Sell a car by Friday, 'kay?" And he was gone before Andy had a chance to reply.

Andy sat back in his chair and began a mental dialogue. *I'm up to the test. I can do this. Three days to sell a car. I can do that.*

That night, Andy discussed his plan for the first time with Lizzy.

"I've never heard of anyone selling cars the way you're going to," she had said. "But maybe that's a good thing. I can't say it doesn't make sense. It sure seems to be more of a personal touch, and I think people like that. I'd love to buy a car that way. I'm curious, though, why you're bucking the system, as you business types would say."

Andy told her about his last four days at Mainstreet Motors, about how confrontational it was, how much of a struggle it was to fit in well enough to perform in a way that made use of his strengths.

"I don't mind a challenge," explained Andy. "It would be easy to walk away. But that's not me. I made a commitment. I know I can make it

69

work. I know I can sell cars—I just have to figure out how."

Lizzy listened attentively before offering her thoughts.

"You're under enormous stress," she said. "And I think I know why."

"Okay, Dr. Harmon, I'll bite," grinned Andy. "Why?"

"Because the inside doesn't match the outside," began Lizzy. "You're out of sorts . . . your rhythm is off. There's a mismatch going on. There's no balanced harmony, no *kyosei*."

"Great, another Zen K word," groaned Andy. "Why is it I've never heard of all this stuff and suddenly it's all around?"

Andy told Lizzy about Axel Simpson and how the practices of genchi genbutsu, hansei, and hoshin all relate to kaizen.

"Well," answered Lizzy, "I think people want to help you through this time of transition and change. So it all relates to your situation and your new direction. It's about maintaining your continuity through change, if that makes sense. And these are age-old philosophies, principles, and practices."

"I'm getting that," said Andy. "So back to your theory."

"I don't know," said Lizzy. "I just think we all have this, what? True Self? True Person? That's how I think of it, anyway. And your True Person has two parts. There's the Internal Person, and the External Person. The External Person is the one you show to others. Maybe it's your game face, your armor, your mask, whatever. It could be your behaviors or even your techniques. But what keeps the External Person going and makes it work is the Internal Person, because I believe we create ourselves from the inside out. The Internal Person is the person inside the persona. But what causes all the stress and tension is when the two don't match. What I've been getting from Mariko is that the ultimate goal is to pursue kyosei, the point of harmony, where the Internal and External Person hold each other in perfect balance, they match, and they're really the same. That's the True Person. You may never reach that point entirely, but you get stronger as you get closer and closer."

"WYSIWYG," said Andy.

"Sorry?" said Lizzy.

"What You See Is What You Get," replied Andy. "Computer term."

"Right," Lizzy replied. "So you're all out of whack because when you were at Mega Box you were closer to that balance point."

Andy was quiet, thinking about what Lizzy had said.

"I want you to come with me to yoga tomorrow night," she said. "We'll get a sitter for the kids. I know you've never tried it, but it may be just what you need right now. Not only physically, but mentally and even spiritually."

"I don't know," wavered Andy. "I feel like I'm already stretched as it is. I have a lot on my mind."

"My point entirely," countered Lizzy. "There's some stuff we do that helps quiet the mind. It's not all just stretching. In the meantime, come to think of it, I know someone at school who wants a new car."

Andy's first call Wednesday morning was to the assistant principal of Twin Falls Jr./Sr. High School. Lizzy had given Andy her information and made the initial introduction. Unfortunately, she was leaving for a conference early the next week and would not be able to meet with Andy until the weekend after.

Somewhat disappointed but not completely discouraged, Andy began his phone campaign. By noon that day he had made nearly thirty calls, leaving messages, talking to people, and trying to set appointments. It wasn't going quite as well as he had hoped. People were surprised to be hearing from a dealership about new cars. Fortunately for Andy, he was able to set two appointments for the afternoon.

One of them has to come through! Or so he hoped.

But it wasn't in the cards for Andy Harmon to sell an automobile that day. One appointment simply didn't show; the other, a long-time customer of the dealership, just wasn't quite ready to buy a car that day. Andy took heart in the fact that the basis for a solid relationship had been formed, and he was confident that a sale would be made in the near future.

Grady Carver was nowhere to be found that afternoon, but his words still rang in Andy's ears: *You have to try a lot harder. Push it, man, push it.*

Heading home that evening, Andy had a looming sense of dread that the coming weekend might be a repeat of the last. If his fears came true, he knew he would have to abandon his long-term plan in favor of making a sale. He had to do whatever it took. His survival depended on it.

Andy was quiet as he and Lizzy drove to The Dojo for Lizzy's Wednesday evening adult yoga class. He felt a little apprehensive about adding yet another new thing to his already overloaded agenda. On the other hand, maybe it would take his mind off his troubles, at least for a while.

"You know," Lizzy started, "I was thinking that maybe you're trying too hard. People can feel it when you're tense, pushing—when you're not confident, and you're trying to overcompensate. Maybe you need to back off and try easy."

"Maybe," Andy replied.

"I remember reading about an Olympic team in the late 1980s," Lizzy continued. "The story goes that there are these ten world-class sprinters all vying for the three remaining qualifying spots for the Olympic trials. They're tight and tense in the first practice heat, because the stakes are so high in this particular meet, and they've been working all their lives on dreams of making the Olympic team. The coach checks his stopwatch, the times are poor. But instead of showing disappointment, he informs them that they'll be timed again in fifteen minutes. But this time, he tells them not to run flat out, go at about 90 percent."

"Okaaayyyy . . . ," Andy interjected. "Let the other shoe drop."

"Every sprinter ran faster the second time," Lizzy concluded. "One runner's time set an official world record. The pressure in the first trial had caused them to tighten up. The coach relieved the pressure in the second race. Point being, try easy."

"Mm," Andy muttered. "Maybe I can introduce Grady Carver to that coach. But I get your drift. I'm putting a lot of pressure on myself. Good counsel."

"We're almost there," Lizzy smiled. "Got another one; want to hear it?"

"Sure," replied Andy.

"This one's about a fly," Lizzy went on.

"A fly?"

"Mm-hmm. This particular fly is buzzing against the window, knocking itself out in a life-or-death

75

struggle, trying to break free. It keeps banging itself against the window to no avail. But it keeps trying harder and harder to fly through the glass through pure effort and determination."

"Happens all the time!" Andy chuckled. "It's natural."

"Right," Lizzy affirmed. "But in this case there's an open door ten steps away, seconds away in flying time. Freedom without all the effort is right there. The fly will die trying its current way."

"But it makes sense to the fly to just keep at it," concluded Andy. "It doesn't even consider other ways because the goal is right there in front of it. It can see it."

"Point being . . . ," Lizzy nodded encouragingly.

"Bzzz, bzzz," finished Andy. "I get it, I get it. That's actually why I'm bucking the store system a bit. But even there maybe I'm pushing it a bit."

"We're here," said Lizzy, changing the subject as they pulled into the parking lot of the small courtyard complex that housed The Dojo and a few other small businesses. "But we're a little early. Mariko holds her advanced adult aikido class right before yoga, and I like to sneak in and watch."

As they entered The Dojo, they did catch the tail end of Mariko's advanced class. She was in the throes of a mock street attack, defending herself against four attackers. They surrounded her at four corners of a square, dwarfing her.

Then Mariko barked a short command, and they all attacked at once. They never knew what hit them. Andy and Lizzy stood off to the side, mesmerized, as Mariko—with a barely perceptible move—was suddenly on the outside of the four. The four attackers kept rushing Mariko, trying to strike or grab or overpower her. Each of their attempts was quickly countered with moves and throws and sweeps that left them down on the mat, wondering how they got there. Where they were clumsy, she was graceful. It was as if Mariko was able to absorb the force of their attack and take command of that energy, moving with it, bending it back on them rather than fighting against it. The ease and efficiency and effectiveness of her movements were coupled with surprising impact and power.

"She looks like she's floating," Lizzy whispered.

"Effortless," Andy whispered back.

> When nothing seems to help, I go and look at a stonecutter hammering away at his rock perhaps a hundred times without as much as a crack showing in it. Yet at the hundred and first blow it will split in two, and I know it was not that blow that did it, but all that had gone before.
>
> —JACOB RIIS

One by one Mariko dispatched her opponents, until only one was left standing face-to-face with her.

"Hit my nose with your fist as hard as you can," she ordered.

The last man struck without hesitation. But his fist never touched her, and he was suddenly on the mat, with Mariko in firm control of his wrist. She let him up, and the Harmons couldn't help but clap.

"I did not see you there!" smiled Mariko, giving a short bow. "Thank you."

"That was amazing," exclaimed Lizzy. "That last move, how ever did you do that?"

"*Win chun,*" answered Mariko, with a quick grin. "Invented by a woman."

"Aha!" cried Lizzy, giving Andy a gentle elbow to the ribs.

"You made it all look so easy," Andy said. "But I know it isn't."

"The Italians call that *sprezzatura,*" informed Lizzy. "The art of making difficult things look easy."

Mariko was smiling, nodding. *"Shibumi!"*

"I love the way that sounds," laughed Lizzy. "Shibumi! So fun . . . I can't say it without smiling."

"What's it mean?" asked Andy.

"It is the Zen term for what you are talking about," began Mariko. "It is a word without literal translation, because I do not know of a single word in English that captures the essence, but it means effortless effectiveness and elegant simplicity and understated beauty. It is the ability to produce the maximum effect through minimum means.

"When you see a problem cleverly solved in a way that makes you slap your forehead and cry 'Of course! How else could it be?' When something has been designed really well, with an understated, effortless beauty, and it really works, that's shibumi.

"My father would say, 'To do without doing, act without acting, think without thinking, this is shibumi.' It is not necessarily something that is achieved, but rather discovered, or perhaps arrived at. It may take many forms, and appears differently depending upon the sphere. It is one thing in the garden, another in architecture, and yet another in the composition of a life. It is more about being and becoming than about doing or achieving. I consider it the height of personal excellence."

79

Andy looked glum. "Well, that's the exact oppo-site of everything I've been about these last two weeks. For me it's been like the minimum effect with the maximum means. Actually, zero effect with excessive means might be more accurate."

Mariko considered Andy's comments, giving him an appraising look. She glanced at Lizzy, and a sparkle appeared in her eyes. "We have a few minutes before class starts. Come with me."

Lizzy and Andy dutifully followed Mariko out into the small courtyard. Mariko led them to the back, stopping at a far corner. There, a small patch stood apart from the rest of the landscaping. "Welcome to my garden," gestured Mariko.

"What are you growing?" asked Andy.

"Nothing," Mariko replied. "More accurately, nothingness. This is a traditional Japanese friend-ship garden. It is called *niwa*, which means 'pure place.' Not unlike the Garden of Eden. Tell me, what do you see?"

Lizzy remained quiet. She knew Mariko was delivering a lesson.

"Rocks, some little stepping stones, gravel with some lines drawn in it," Andy replied immediately. "Nothing much, actually. No flowers!"

"Look closer," urged Mariko. "Describe the nature of what you see."

Andy scratched his head. "Well, there's nothing much to it. Pretty simple."

"Yes, Andy-san," Mariko replied. "This is the aesthetic principle of simplicity, or *kanso*. As you say, rocks, stones, and that is sea gravel. That is all. No flowers or bushes planted. Kanso reminds us that beauty need not be overstated, or ornate, or decorative, or embellished. In fact, the principle of *koko*, or austerity, is a complementary concept. Koko is the subtraction of all but the bare essentials."

"Come to think of it," Andy went on, "it's mostly empty."

"You are exactly right," said Mariko. "You see, as the Zen philosophy took root in Japan over eight hundred years ago, Japanese art and philosophy began to reflect one of the fundamental Zen aesthetic themes: emptiness. But long before that, the Chinese philosopher Lao Tzu, who lived roughly in the same time as Daruma, wrote a verse in his book *Tao Te Ching* that goes 'Thirty spokes share the wheel's hub, it is the center hole that makes it useful. Shape clay into a vessel, it is the space within that makes it useful. Cut doors and windows for a room, it is the holes which make it useful. Therefore profit comes from what is there, usefulness from what is not there.'"

"That's an interesting way of looking at things," Andy said. "Unique, actually."

"Yes," Mariko went on, nodding, "You see, in the Zen view, emptiness is a symbol of inexhaustible spirit. It takes many forms. Silent pauses in music and theater, blank spaces in paintings, and even the restrained motion of a geisha pouring tea. These all have a special significance because it is in states of temporary inactivity or quietude that Zen artists see the very essence of creative energy. This is the principle of *seijaku*."

"If I'm being totally honest, it's sort of lopsided. I mean, there are some rocks there, but none there in that big space," said Andy, pointing.

"Ah," smiled Mariko. "You noticed. The goal of the Zen artist is to convey the symmetrical harmony and beauty of nature through clearly asymmetrical and incomplete renderings; the effect is that those viewing the art supply the missing symmetry and thus participate in the act of creation. This is called *fukinsei*."

"But the lines and grooves in the gravel," observed Andy, "are evenly spaced. The concentric circles around

Life comes in clusters, clusters of solitude, then clusters when there is hardly time to breathe.

–MAY SARTON

that rock, for example. They look like ripples in the water when you drop a pebble."

"Yes," confirmed Mariko, "but it is the rock that interrupts the pattern of the lines. This signifies break from routine, or habit, or normalcy. The lines may be taken to represent convention, the rock surprises the viewer because it breaks the pattern. It is meant to be a surprise and may be thought of as freedom from burdensome restriction and regulation. Some say that it is the seed bed of ultimate creativity. This is the principle of *datsuzoku*."

"Mariko, this is all so fascinating," said Lizzy. "And so minimal, yet so naturally beautiful. Raw but refined. It is spare, but it is the austerity that makes it so, I don't know, purposeful, intentionally authentic?"

Mariko gave a little bow, saying, "Thank you. To be viewed in this way, as without pretense, without artifice, not forced, yet to be seen as intentional, not

83

born of accident, this is a high compliment. The power of the garden lies in part with this paradox. It takes great care to achieve this balance between at once being of nature yet distinct from it. This is the principle of *shizen*."

"So," Andy said slowly, "I'm getting that while at first it looks random, there is a hint of an order to things, but it's meant to suggest, not bang you over the head with any one thing. Not everything is spelled out. Like over on that side, you can't see the whole rock, it's partially hidden from view. It makes you want to step along the path to see more . . ."

"That is astute of you, Andy-san!" cried Mariko. "Yes, yes, yes. Because Zen Buddhists view the human spirit as by nature indefinable, the power of suggestion is exalted as the mark of a truly authentic creation. Finiteness is thought to be at odds with nature, implying stagnation, loss of life. This is the principle of *yugen.* Be subtle, leave things open to interpretation, and the recipients are more engaged. They in fact become creators themselves."

"I believe Leonardo da Vinci held a similar view," offered Lizzy. "His technique was *sfumato,* which literally translates to 'like smoke,' which Leonardo defined as 'without having distinct edges and lines.'"

"Please go on," urged Mariko. "I did not know this!"

"So with sfumato," explained Lizzy, "the lines are left a little vague, and forms are slightly blurred to merge with one another. This is why Leonardo's paintings were so lifelike. The reason the Mona Lisa is so alluring and captivating is that the corners of her eyes and mouth, which are the two features responsible for human expression, are deliberately indistinct, blurry. She seems to be alive because her attitude is so open to interpretation."

"Yugen!" Mariko gave a little gleeful clap of her hands, clearly enjoying Lizzy's discourse.

"And," Lizzy finished, "Leonardo actually advised his students to leave something to the imagination. He said that sfumato leads the observer to understand what one does not see."

"So when I look at this garden, or at the Mona Lisa," interrupted Andy, "I'm actually completing the picture, as it were?"

Lizzy and Mariko answered at the same time. "Yes!"

"I really wish I had bought a journal," Andy stated. "Like Ax told me to. I need to write all this down."

"That would be good," smiled Mariko, nodding. "I will write these down for you. These seven aesthetic qualities can guide the design of nearly everything, no matter if it is an action or an object. I call upon them to shape my life, to guide me in selecting the techniques I choose to teach, and to provide a framework for how I wish to build my business. Although I can describe them all individually, in truth they cannot be separated from each other. They all are intertwined and connected. I call them 'the shibumi seven.'

"Kanso, simplicity.

"Koko, austerity and subtraction of the non-essential.

"Seijaku, quietude and stillness.

"Fukinsei, asymmetry and seductive imperfection.

"Datsuzoku, break from convention.

"Shizen, naturalness without pretense or artifice.

"Yugen, subtlety and suggestion.

"Taken together with the other principles and practices we have discussed, they help me not only understand the concept of shibumi in a meaningful way, but provide pathways for pursuing it."

Mariko then announced that it was finally time for the yoga class. As they returned to The Dojo, Lizzy whispered to Andy. "Funny how all these things tie together with what we were talking about in the car. Pulling back, not pushing, trying easy . . . less is best."

"Mm," Andy murmured, thinking. The thought running through his mind was: *Easy to understand, not so easy to achieve.*

Andy didn't exactly know what to expect from his first experience with yoga, but it was much harder than he had imagined. Mariko put the four men and nine women attending the class through a series of progressively more difficult positions, many of which Andy could not do. Andy used muscles he didn't even know he had, and came to the realization at the end that he had completed a rigorous physical workout.

Mariko concluded the class with a short mindful awareness meditation session in which she instructed the class to sit on their mats cross-legged, rest their hands in their laps, close their eyes, and focus all of their attention simply on their breathing, nothing else.

"The goal," Mariko said, "is to learn to be still, to not think, to quiet the mind and free it from conscious thought. Try to observe yourself simply sitting and breathing. To just be, that is Zen."

It was impossible, though, for Andy to stop thinking. His mind kept wandering forward to what the next few days held for him.

The drive home was an unusually quiet one. Lizzy seemed completely relaxed and refreshed, but by the time they arrived home, it was all Andy could do to tumble into bed, exhausted.

When it goes wrong, you feel like cutting your throat, but you go on. You don't let anything get you down so much that it beats you or stops you.

−GEORGE CUKOR

The next few days at Mainstreet Motors proved to be uneventful for Andy, at least in terms of making a sale. With every customer, he knew he was getting a little better. He followed his hoshin, and made sure to conduct his hansei after each encounter. Kaizen was alive and well in his activities.

Andy tried to keep in mind all the new principles that he had learned Wednesday evening in Mariko's garden. He kept thinking about the pursuit of shibumi, and all the supporting Zen aesthetic principles. Mariko had counseled him to avoid direct application of them for the time being, and to simply keep them rumbling around in back of his mind. They were difficult and many, and certainly nowhere near feeling natural or intuitive.

"Keep them close in mind," Mariko had advised. "There will come a point in time and place where their invocation will be appropriate. You will know it. Do not force them at this point. Think of them as ways and avenues along which to pursue shibumi through kaizen, as roads and means by which to constantly improve. They cannot be viewed as techniques at this point, merely guides to your approach."

I have got *to get a journal*, Andy reminded himself.

In the days following, no matter how hard he tried, Andy could not close a sale. No matter what he did, he could not move past the demonstration drive part of the sales process. For some reason, he could not reach an agreement with a potential customer to engage in a purchase proposal discussion and enter into the transaction phase. He was able to overcome objections. He was able to answer questions about model features and benefits with confidence. He was able to establish rapport, to connect with prospective customers. He was able to secure promises to call, promises to return, and even set future appointments to continue the dialogue. But he could not, try as he might, sell a car in one encounter. There was promise of future business, but the waiting was causing stress.

Andy's fears came true that weekend. He had decided to work another Sunday, after Saturday proved fruitless. It had been over two weeks, and his third weekend at the dealership.

Grady Carver had been too busy to give Andy any time or attention. But at noon on Sunday, he once more arrived at Andy's desk.

"Listen, Andy," he began. "I know you're frustrated. Hell, I'm frustrated. You seem to know what you're talking about, according to the rest of the guys. Customers seem to like you. But it's not happening. We both know that. Usually by now, a greenpea has sold at least one unit. I don't have the time to analyze what you're doing wrong, you're gonna have to figure it out for yourself. This keeps up, we're going to have to part ways. I don't mind giving you a little more time. I think I said two units a week within a month. You're over the half-way mark. Results-wise, right now failure is mostly what I'm seeing. I'm seeing no fit. Maybe you need to rethink your decision."

Andy could only listen and nod.

"Go home, take the rest of the day and tomorrow off, come back fresh on Tuesday," continued Grady. "Then give it your absolute best shot. I'm taking the week off myself, but we'll talk again this time next week. And remember, I'm there to help close the deal once you desk it. But you have got to get those numbers on the page first. See ya when I get back. Don't let me down, 'kay?"

Andy had no response. He had no immediate answers. It was all he could do to muster a feeble nod. He was at a loss for what to do. He felt like he had hit some impenetrable wall.

Andy walked out to his car. The doubts, fears, and rationalizations that he had to this point successfully held at bay began to creep into his mind.

A single question burned in his brain: *Did I do the right thing?*

Andy refrained from answering too quickly. He knew better. Experience told him that second-guessing himself probably wouldn't improve the situation any, and might actually make things worse.

"Heading home?" a voice off to Andy's right called out. Axel Simpson. Axel was getting into his car. "Me too. Just came in to grab my notebook I left here yesterday."

"Yessir," Andy said. "Grady sent me home till Tuesday. Glad of it, too. I need a break."

Axel came over. "Been a struggle, huh?"

"Oh yeah . . . ," Andy nodded. "I've learned a lot. From you, Mariko, everyone. Don't get me wrong, it's all good stuff. Great stuff. But I can't seem to close the deal, sell a car."

"Give it time," offered Axel.

"I don't have it to give, that's the problem," countered Andy. "If something doesn't break, if I can't break through this wall I keep hitting my head against, I'm out next week."

"Maybe that's actually what you need," said Axel. "A break, I mean."

"Lizzy thinks I'm trying too hard," agreed Andy. "Pushing too hard."

"Something to that," nodded Axel. "A little datsuzoku. It's all about taking a break from the normal everyday stuff, the stuff you know and expect. Good things happen when you break from habit, break from routine, break from tradition, break from conventional thinking. Hey, I walk down the stairs in my house backward every once in a while, put my pants on right leg first every once in a while just to change it up. You've been through the wringer, man. A temporary departure may be just what the doctor ordered. Little M.I.A. now and then works wonders."

"Everything's pointing that way," said Andy. "I probably just need to back off. Try easy. Get my second wind. Relax, refocus. Recharge the batteries."

> The very greatest things—great thoughts, discoveries, inventions—have usually been nurtured in hardship, often pondered over in sorrow, and at length established with difficulty.
>
> —SAMUEL SMILES

"See ya soon," Axel said, and waved. "Have a good one."

"Yep," Andy answered. "Thanks for all."

Andy drove home, looking forward to spending the afternoon with the family. *I'll take a nice long drive in the country tomorrow. Change of scenery. Stand back from everything. Get a new perspective. No plan, just wander. Surprise myself.*

the breakthrough

And Archimedes, as he was washing, thought of a manner of computing
the proportion of gold in King Hiero's crown by seeing the water
flowing over the bathing-stool. He leaped up as one possessed
or inspired, crying, "I have found it! Eureka!"

−PLUTARCH

Andy arrived home Sunday afternoon after stopping off at the stationer to pick up a journal. Scotty and Sandra and the entire pack of kids from the neighborhood were playing out in the cul de sac, riding bikes, rollerblading, and pushing their scooters around. He dropped his briefcase in the den, glanced up at the Daruma doll, and said under his breath: "Nowhere even close, buddy."

Andy found Lizzy curled up on the couch with a pile of books. "Little light reading?" he quipped.

"Got another ten in the car, funny man," she countered. "I didn't expect you until tonight! Everything okay?"

"Couldn't make anything work at the store," Andy said. "Grady sent me home until Tuesday. Not looking real good. I need a break."

Lizzy remained silent for a moment, appraising him. Then, "Meaning physical, mental, or both?"

"Meaning all of the above," Andy replied. "I was thinking of taking a long drive out in the country tomorrow. Just me, no plan, no direction, other than away from town."

"That sounds really good," agreed Lizzy. "Hey, even Bill Gates locks himself away from the world now and then. Maybe it'll work for you."

"Okay, I'll bite," teased Andy, flopping down next to Lizzy. "What are you talking about?"

"'Think Week.' Pretty legendary, mister business-man," she ribbed back. "Bill Gates holes up twice a year in a secret hideaway, a tiny lakeside cottage somewhere near Seattle. Supposedly he ponders the past, present, and future of Microsoft, of technology, and of the computer industry. He reads hundreds of white papers submitted by employees, takes long walks, contemplates the wins and losses, successes and failures."

"That's hansei," Andy concluded. "And that's sort of what I was thinking. But I was also thinking about, er, not thinking. I think I have reality vertigo. Too much has happened and not happened all at once. Too much, not enough, too soon. I keep coming up against a brick wall."

Lizzy chuckled.

"Not funny," Andy muttered. "It's pretty sad."

"No, no, no," Lizzy quickly corrected. "I was just thinking I know how you feel. And I was remembering this story my dad told me when I was in college. He was driving me home for the winter break. For the entire semester I had been banging my head against the wall in my physics class. I just couldn't wrap my brain around some of the concepts. I thought I was going to maybe fail my winter exams, maybe even the course."

"That does sound like me," Andy said.

"Right," nodded Lizzy. "So, we're driving home; I'm explaining my woes about this one particular set of concepts. My father had been a physics major, but rather than just give me some tricks of the trade, so to speak, he told me a story."

"Would have loved to have been in the back seat for that!" Andy laughed, adding, "I'm sure that made you happy!"

"Oh yeah, not really," Lizzy confirmed. "I was a little put out, you could say. So anyway, it's a story about this farmer who comes across a huge boulder when clearing his fields. No matter how hard he tries, the farmer cannot push the massive stone off the field. Over and over again he tries to push it off. This way, that way. It's taking all his energy and stealing his enthusiasm. The boulder won't budge. The farmer can't plant his crops with it in the way, and he's at a complete loss, fretting, mourning his predicament, and paralyzed by his bad luck. He's becoming desperate. Throwing his hands up in surrender, he walks away and goes to the well for a cool drink of water and to take a breather."

"He gave up?" Andy asked.

"Just wait, I'm not done!" cried Lizzy. "The farmer is at the well, peering down into the dark hole. Suddenly inspiration hits him: Hole! The farmer races to his shed, grabs a shovel and a plank for a lever, and returns to the field. He digs a deep hole around, under and in front of the boulder and tips it into the hole."

"Brilliant," commented Andy.

"Slap to your forehead brilliant, right?" Lizzy replied. "Then the farmer covers the rock with dirt. And from that day on, the farmer stood each day on the spot where he'd buried the boulder. What had been his biggest barrier had now become part of his very foundation."

"Your father thought this helped you . . . how?" Andy looked puzzled.

"His way of telling me something," Lizzy replied. "His message about the farmer was to take a break, get away from it."

"'Break' is a big part of breakthrough," Andy finished.

"Yep," nodded Lizzy. "Literally and scientifically. Don't you always get your best and most creative ideas when you're doing something else . . . taking a shower, daydreaming, driving, sleeping, taking a walk? I know I do."

"True enough," Andy nodded.

"Don't forget," Lizzy said. "Einstein got his theory of special relativity in a daydream."

"That's good news," quipped Andy, "since all I want to do is sell a car."

Lizzy giggled. "His problem was as tough for him as yours is for you. There's lots of stories about brilliant flashes of insight that came at strange times and in random locations. They didn't occur while actually working on the problem but after an intense, prolonged struggle with it followed by a

> I have always fought for ideas—until I learned that it isn't ideas but grief, struggle, and flashes of vision which enlighten.
>
> —MARGARET ANDERSON

break. A change of scene and time away seem to have played a part."

"There's hope for me yet!" Andy smiled. He thought a moment, and a more serious look came over his face. "What did you mean, though, when you said *scientifically?*"

"Well, the research is pretty clear," Lizzy answered. "I think most creative types like artists, writers, musicians probably know instinctively that their work involves seemingly unproductive times."

"Like writer's block," offered Andy.

"Right," nodded Lizzy. "But they also know those downtimes and time-outs are important ingredients of immensely productive and creative periods. There have been a number of recent studies looking into how the human brain solves problems, especially along the lines of what they call 'sudden creative insight.'"

"Meaning . . . ?"

"Those big aha! moments," Lizzy continued. "You know, Archimedes' Eureka! moment in the bathtub, Einstein's daydream. Anyway, what these studies show is that these sudden creative flashes tend to come when the mind is engaged in an activity unrelated to the issue at hand, and that pressure is not conducive to creative thought. Time—time away from the problem and time to quiet the mind—is a key factor."

"Datsuzoko and seijaku," said Andy. "Take a break. Find stillness, calm, and quietude. Zen with scientific support. I like that."

"In fact," Lizzy explained, "one study demonstrated that the ultimate break—sleep—in fact promotes our ability to experience a breakthrough moment. A neuroscientist in Germany gave people some Mensa-type number sequences, and the goal was to find the pattern. He let them struggle with the problem for a while, then gave them a break. One group took naps, the other didn't. Guess what happened?"

"The ones who took the naps came back and solved the problem quicker!" cried Andy.

"And more often," said Lizzy. "What they think happens is that when you sleep, the part of the brain that bundles and repackages memories and fragments of information from other areas does

> I go to my studio every day. Some days the work comes easily. Other days nothing happens. Yet on the good days the inspiration is only an accumulation of all the other days, the nonproductive ones.
>
> —BEVERLY PEPPER

its thing and then sends them to the part of the brain that synthesizes them into higher-level thought. And that enables your brain to clear itself and, in effect, reboot, all the while forming new connections and associations. They know that this process is the foundation for creativity, the outcome is new insight and the aha! feeling of the Eureka moment. But . . ."

"But what? I knew there would be a catch!"

"But they don't yet know what that process is," finished Lizzy. "And you're right, it is a pretty obvious catch. If you don't know what it is, you can't speed it up or artificially influence it to work harder or more intensely. Putting pressure on yourself may only slow you down."

"You have to take a break for a breakthrough to occur," Andy concluded.

"You can only let go," nodded Lizzy. "It's rather ironic. When you stop and take a break, somehow escape, either mentally or physically, you may actually speed up those magical transformational processes in your mind."

"But," Andy began, thoughtfully, "that raises the question of why we push so hard all the time? And I can't just take a nap at work, and I can't always take a day off. So what are you supposed to do? Sure, try harder, work harder, push harder may not work, and it may do nothing but slow things down. But I'm not likely to take a break unless I'm ordered to, like Grady did."

"Actually, that's not a bad strategy," replied Lizzy. "I was reading about a major management consulting firm that did just that, with some amazing results. They proved you can get better results at work by working less."

"Seriously?" asked Andy, incredulous. "I had friends in Chicago that worked for consulting firms; they put in eighty-hour weeks sometimes. Work first, personal time negligible. It was an 'always on' kind of job."

"It was a whole four-year study," Lizzy said. "In the experiment, consulting teams were required to take predictable, scheduled time off every week, defined as one uninterrupted evening free each week after 6 P.M.—no work contact whatsoever, and no BlackBerrys."

"I have to believe that made people nervous," Andy commented.

"It did," Lizzy affirmed. "The downtime was awkward and even nerve-racking for some, and a few fought the idea, fearful of poor performance ratings or more weekend work."

"Well, yeah," said Andy. "Maybe it's irrational, but there's the fear of failure looming over you. Backing off somehow feels wrong, like preemptive surrender. It's scary to ease up, because you may lose your steam, or you may abandon hope. I get anxious when things aren't going as planned, and I start doubting myself. I'm scared that if I take my eye off the problem even for a moment, I may lose all the energy I've invested."

"But the fact is that without a break, there may just be no breakthrough," argued Lizzy. "So the goal was to teach people that you can tune out completely for a time and still produce great work."

"And?" asked Andy.

"It worked," stated Lizzy. "Company internal surveys showed that within six months, consultants were more satisfied with their jobs and work-life balance, and more likely to stay with the firm, compared to those who weren't part of the study. And their clients told the researchers that the teams turned out better work. They said there was more open dialogue among team members, and that the improved communication also sparked new processes that enhanced the teams' ability to work most efficiently and effectively. It worked so well that they're now rolling out the strategy across the firm."

"May be a while before it catches on at Mainstreet Motors," said Andy.

"There's another way," Lizzy said. "William Ford of Ford Motor does it. Top executives at companies like General Electric, 3M, Google, and Bloomberg do it. Los Angeles Lakers head coach Phil Jackson does it. Elite athletes and teams like Italy's 2006 World Cup champion soccer team do it."

"What's 'it'?" asked Andy.

"Designate daily time to calm and quiet the mind," answered Lizzy.

"How?" asked Andy.

"The way Mariko showed you Wednesday night," Lizzy replied.

"You mean meditation?" asked Andy.

"Mm-hmm."

"The jury's still out on that," said Andy. "Honestly, I'm not sure I have the patience. I know I was supposed to stop thinking, but my brain was chatterboxing away thirty seconds in."

"That's natural. So you have to keep coming to yoga with me!" Lizzy smiled happily. "You've only tried it once, and you need to give it a chance. Just know that mindful awareness meditation may be the most powerful tool known for achieving a stable state of relaxed awareness and alertness. It actually sets the stage for breakthroughs."

"It would be nice if I could turn off my thoughts," agreed Andy. "These last few weeks I've been waking up in the middle of the night, and when I do, my mind is racing. And I can't go back to sleep for hours. But it's the same old loop playing out, which gets me nowhere."

"You know that Daruma doll Mariko gave you?" offered Lizzy. "You remember the story, right? Daruma meditating for years to seek enlightenment. Well, not only are Mariko's meditation instructions those of the ancient Buddhist priests, but Buddhist monks are among the most studied groups in neuroscientific research. For nearly two decades they've been studying Tibetan monks in the hills above Dharamsala to understand how meditation affects brain activity."

"Why?" asked Andy.

"Because," Lizzy went on, "they've discovered using advanced techniques, like electroencephalography, that the most experienced Buddhist practitioners—those with ten thousand hours or more of meditation behind them, called adepts—exhibit abnormally high levels of the exact kind of brainwaves associated with the state of focused awareness thought to immediately precede the Eureka moment."

"So first thing I do, I become a Zen master with ten thousand hours of meditation under my belt," joked Andy. Lizzy shot him a withering look, so he quickly said, "Just kidding. Seriously, their brains are wired differently?"

"From the meditation!" Lizzy nodded. "That means we may actually be able to rewire our brains to adopt different thinking circuits. Not only that, but the whole notion that our thoughts are governed by our brains is being reversed. There's evidence that how and what you think, or not think, may actually alter the physical structure of our gray matter. They call the phenomenon *neuroplasticity.*"

"In other words," Andy finished, "if you quiet your mind, you can change your brain, and almost engineer a breakthrough."

A quiet mind cureth all.
  –ROBERT BURTON

"Your brain needs the calm before its storm," smiled Lizzy.

Monday morning rolled around, and when Lizzy and the kids had finally left for school, Andy loaded up his daypack, complete with food, a book, and his journal, and headed out toward the rolling green hills and farmlands surrounding Twin Falls. He was hoping that the getaway, especially on his own, would help him clear his head. It had been quite awhile since he had explored the countryside. He knew that life out here was quite different from that of the town. At the very least he'd get a new perspective. Andy wanted to sit by the waterfalls, relax, think, review his situation, and maybe even conduct a little hansei, and balance it all with a little not thinking, a little seijaku. Maybe he'd try to meditate. The day would be without structure. He would take it as it came and go with the flow.

It didn't take long before town was disappearing in his rearview mirror. The countryside was spectacular; white picket fences, expansive fields of corn and alfalfa, quaint farmhouses and siloed barns. Horses, cattle, sheep. For a quick moment, Andy allowed himself to entertain the notion of becoming a farmer. Fresh air, outdoors, away from fluorescent lights. Physical work would feel great. Up at dawn, asleep at dusk. No cell phones. Self-sufficiency. The simple life.

Before the fact that he knew nothing about farming had a chance to creep in from the left side of his brain, Andy's reverie was shattered by a man with a broken-down truck on the side of the road, waving him down.

Might as well do my good deed for the day, Andy thought as he pulled over on the dirt shoulder. *That truck's gotta be at least twenty-five years old. No wonder he has trouble.*

From the looks of him, the man was obviously a farmer. Andy got out and walked toward him.

The man was already approaching Andy, hand outstretched.

"Howdy, friend," he began. "I do thank you. Ezekiel Barker's my name. Friends call me Zeke. This old beast is having a bad day."

"Andy Harmon," replied Andy, smiling and returning the handshake. "Not sure I can help, but I can at least give you a lift. What's wrong, do you think?"

"Old age, mostly," smiled Zeke. "Just sorta conked out on me. Not the first time either. Last time it was the alternator."

"How many miles on her?" asked Andy, lifting the hood.

"Coupla hundred thousand on a rebuild. Had her since '74."

"No kidding!" cried Andy. "Don't know many people keep a car that long."

"Then you ain't from around here," said Zeke. "Must be a townie. Near all of us out here do. I got four vehicles, all at least ten years old. This one's the oldest, though. Good long life, she's been good to me."

Andy closed the hood and wiped his hands. "I'm not sure what's wrong. I think we'll have to get a tow truck to come get her. She's not going anywhere on her own."

Then Zeke's last comment sank in. "Really?" asked Andy, shaking his head in disbelief. "How come? Keep a car that long, I mean."

Zeke shrugged. "New stuff's expensive, loses half the value once you buy. Probably not built as good anymore. Lotta fancy gizmos and such. Confusing. Mostly, though, we hate goin' inta them dealerships. Don't like doin' business with folks we don't know. And it ain't like they make house calls. Sorta skeptical of townsfolk in general. Always seem in a rush. Chasing the big dollar, I guess. You seem okay, though."

"All good points, especially the last," chuckled Andy.

Zeke was smiling.

And suddenly, without warning, everything clicked into place.

This is it!

A million thoughts were racing through his head. *Match made in heaven! There must be at least a hundred farms around Twin Falls, maybe two. Three, four cars each. They hate dealerships as much as I do. Forget selling new cars, sell them previously owned certified ones. Better for them, better for me. Come out here and do it. It's a fleet sale! Get to know everyone, build a business on relationships. What if I acted as a broker, almost? Why not? Slow down—think! How would this work? Don't push. Observe first. Keep it simple. Be yourself. Leave it open.*

All of the ill-fated planning, the practice, the struggle, and all of the many principles and practices that had come into his life in the past few weeks, were in preparation for this single encounter. Mariko's words came back to him, *there will be a time and place . . . you will know.* That time and place was now. Andy could feel it in his bones.

"All makes sense to me," commented Andy, with a shrug. "Come on, let's get to a station and get this old beauty home."

As they drove, Andy began asking Zeke questions. *Genchi genbutsu.* What kind of farming did he do? What was it like to be a farmer? What was the farming community all about? What was his family like?

"You sure are the inquiring type," said Zeke, finally. "What about yourself?"

Andy told him his story. About moving to Twin Falls. About Lizzy and the kids. About Mega Box. Finally, Andy talked about his new job. He kept the story simple, spare, and without any pretense. *Kanso. Koko. Shizen.*

"Well, you don't seem much like no car huckster I ever met," Zeke commented, chuckling. "Ya seem too much a regular guy. Not all huffy and fake."

"Thanks, I think," laughed Andy.

"What kinda trucks they buildin' nowadays, anyway?" asked Zeke. "Looks like I might be in the market."

Two shoe salesmen were sent to Africa in the early 1900s to scout the territory. One telegraphed back: "Situation hopeless. Stop. No one wears shoes." The other telegraphed: "Business opportunity. Stop. They have no shoes."

—ANONYMOUS

"See for yourself," Andy said, jerking his thumb toward the back seat, where the corners of a few brochures on the new full ton pickup line were peeking out from under his jacket.

Zeke looked a little skeptical, hesitant. Finally curiosity overcame him, and he reached back to grab the brochures and began leafing through them. *Yugen*, Andy thought.

"Listen, I think I have an idea that could make life easier for you," began Andy, as Zeke thumbed through the brochure. "What if I come back out here, say on Wednesday evening. Forget the brand new truck for now. We have some used ones, late model, coupla years old only, a third the price of new, pretty much the same body and style you see there, fully inspected and warrantied. I'll bring one out to you. You can drive it around, check it out nine ways from Sunday. All in the comfort of your own place. You like it, it's yours. You hate it, I scram."

"You'd do that?" asked Zeke, incredulously. "That's a kindly offer. Heck, that's a deal."

Zeke stuck out his hand, and Andy gave it a firm handshake.

"Be my pleasure," replied Andy. "It's beautiful out here. And the people are friendly!"

"Well, okay then!" chuckled Zeke. "And Wednesday's good," he smiled, as if confirming the date for himself. "Fact, some of the boys'll be there. Poker night. Now then, if you turn right here and go down about a mile, we got Jethro's Garage."

Andy never finished his day in the country. After exchanging important information and leaving Zeke at Jethro's, Andy couldn't wait to get back to the store and get things in order. Never in a million years would he have thought to sell cars off-site to the farming "market." It was a huge opportunity, and he wanted to make sure he capitalized on it. He wanted to bring Zeke the best full-size truck they had on the used lot, make sure it was okay legally, and get all the paperwork ready just in case Zeke wanted to buy it. That meant a credit check, too. And he wanted to see if there was anything they could do for Zeke in the way of taking care of his antique pickup. And he wanted to do a bit of homework to determine just how extensive the farming community was, and what the potential market might be, vehicle-wise. He wanted to make sure he had the entire used truck inventory detailed with pictures and specs, just in case someone else showed interest Wednesday evening. He had a lot to do to make sure everything went smoothly.

As he pulled into the Mainstreet Motors employee lot, he passed Axel Simpson heading back from the Parts Department. Andy waved. Axel stopped and waited for Andy to approach.

"Thought you had the day off?" he asked. "You look different, too. Happy, almost."

"I did, I do, I am," Andy retorted with a smile. He hadn't felt this good in weeks. The promise of the day was showing on his face.

Axel put one hand on his hip, and rubbed his chin with the other. "Hmm. Something good obviously happened. Care to share?"

And so Andy told Axel everything that had happened that day. Axel listened, nodding and grinning. When Andy finished, Axel uttered a single word: *"Hirameki!"*

"That's a good thing, right?" Andy grinned.

"Sudden insight, breakthrough moment," nodded Axel. "This is huge. When it's right, it's right. Don't just stand here jabbering with me, get to it!"

Axel was off, and Andy on his way.

At four-thirty on Wednesday afternoon, Andy headed out toward Zeke's farm, driving the vehicle he thought Zeke would like most. As he pulled into the courtyard in front of the farmhouse, Andy was surprised at the number of cars that were parked there. He counted ten. Some big poker night they do, he thought. Greeting him at the door was a woman that could only be Zeke's wife.

"You must be Andy," she said, holding open the screen door. "I'm Betsy, and they're all waiting for you in the parlor. Zeke hasn't stopped talking about you for two days. You saved his life, to listen to him."

"It's nice to meet you, ma'am. I just gave him a lift is all." Andy shrugged.

"Well, truth be told, we wouldn't expect it from city folk. Not that we have a big city, mind you, but you know what I mean."

Andy smiled and nodded.

"There he is!" boomed Zeke, as Andy entered the room. Zeke was pumping his hand like a long-lost friend, introducing him around.

Andy felt like he was at a surprise birthday party for himself. He was an instant celebrity to the group in the room. *And I haven't done a thing!* Andy thought.

For the next two hours Andy was a one-man show, all energy and enthusiasm. He answered questions about the truck. He told about what the dealership offered in the way of service. He talked about all the various models they had, both new models and certified previously owned vehicles. Everyone took a turn at driving the truck, Andy talking and explaining all the while.

By the time the poker game was about to begin, Andy had not only sold Zeke the truck, he'd also taken five more orders for the same model, set four appointments to come back out, and, most important, become one of them.

They seemed to trust him. And not just about cars. They asked him about financial issues. They asked him about local politics. It was as if he was a conduit to the town, to "urban" life, a vital connection between two very different ways of life.

It was a whole new world for Andy, something he thought might go well beyond selling cars. The fact

Guess how I made that head of a bull. One day, in a rubbish heap, I found an old bicycle seat, lying beside a rusted handlebar . . . and my mind instantly linked them together. The idea came to me before I even realized it. I just soldered them together.

–PABLO PICASSO

remained, though, that Andy had far surpassed his immediate goal, exceeded his plan, and gone far beyond anything he had planned for, hoped for, or even imagined. He sensed he was approaching the cradle of shibumi.

He had broken through.

the transformation

Opportunities to find deeper powers within ourselves come when life seems most challenging; we must be willing to get rid of the life we've planned, so as to have the life that is waiting for us. When we quit thinking primarily about ourselves and our own self-preservation, we undergo a truly heroic transformation of consciousness.

–JOSEPH CAMPBELL

Andy barely remembered dialing the phone in the Barkers' kitchen and calling Lizzy to come pick him up. He was floating on air as they drove home, with Scotty and Sandra fast asleep in the back seat. As they drove, Andy recounted the evening, still in disbelief and trying to figure out what it meant.

And it was Lizzy who helped him make sense of the experience.

"Don't you see? You were helping others, and that's why you sold cars. They viewed you as a leader, someone helping them solve a problem, giving them helpful information, making their lives easier. It had nothing to do with your product. They needed you—they just didn't quite know it until you appeared."

It wasn't about selling cars, Lizzy explained. In fact, it wasn't about cars at all. It was about people. Connecting with them, meeting their needs. *Serving,* not *selling.*

A new realization dawned on Andy: *I'm using my strengths to help others succeed.* He said as much to Lizzy.

"That should be your *mantra,*" she told him. "It is your simple but deep statement of belief, of purpose, of both cause and contribution. It is what creates meaning, in your life and in the lives of others."

"Certainly a much better reason to get out of bed in the morning," Andy mused.

From that moment on, a world of possibility opened for Andy. His mind raced with ideas that had little to do with his job task. He could talk to Betsy's book club, talk to them about automobile safety and maintenance. He could talk to the Rotary Club, talk to them about financing strategies. He could help Zeke and the farming community by helping them plan out what made sense for their businesses in terms of vehicles and equipment.

He could connect the farming community with all kinds of service providers in town who could help them get ahead—tax advisers, financial planners, accountants, lawyers, computer consultants.

As he lay in bed mulling over the events of the past few weeks—the old door that had closed behind him and the new door that had just opened—Andy had the distinct feeling that an altogether new chapter in his life was unfolding, a shift in direction that he had never prepared for, or even envisioned. He acknowledged to himself that he couldn't possibly have seen it from the beginning, and that the steps leading up to his moment of breakthrough were all necessary, and all played a meaningful part in some bigger plan.

Above all, it seemed to Andy at this point that nothing was impossible. It was, he realized, a point of departure. And the destination was shibumi.

> In the time we have it is surely our duty to do all the good we can to all the people we can in all the ways we can.
>
> —WILLIAM BARCLAY

Andy never did sell a car in the Mainstreet Motors store. In the days and weeks that followed, he experienced an awakening, the emergence of a new identity—at his place of employment, in his home life, and in the community.

Grady Carver was pleasantly surprised to learn of Andy's activities. In fact, once Andy had relayed the goings-on, Grady seemed to have a newfound interest in what Andy was planning, asking lots of questions, but not to the point of second-guessing Andy. Meeting the immediate sales objective was no longer an issue, so Grady was content to let the matter ride, at least for now. In his view, it didn't much matter how a car got sold, as long as the metal moved off the lot. More power to anyone who can open up a whole new market, like it seemed Andy had done.

Because Andy's plan was now directed outward to the surrounding farming community, it didn't make much sense to keep his desk at the dealership. He moved his operation into the spare bedroom at home. Lizzy and the kids were gone most of the day, so setting up shop to work out of the house was perfect. By the time everyone came home from school, Andy was out on calls. Grady Carver didn't seem to have a problem with Andy working from his home, as long as all the paperwork was done right. Andy still came in to the store once a week to deliver retail contracts, but he became a whiz at the kitchen-table deal. He even brought Grady along every once in a while to meet his clients.

The rest of the sales team could only marvel at their "traveling salesman," as they called Andy. They began asking Andy's advice on how to be more proactive, and how to think about building a long-term referral business. Andy taught them how to mine their past sales. He taught them how to use the telephone to set appointments. He taught them how to be more customer-focused, how to pull rather than push. And when it was appropriate, he taught them the principles and concepts that had helped him transform his life.

Slowly, but surely, Mainstreet Motors took on a new personality. Andy worked closely with Axel Simpson, who led the charge in instilling practices like kaizen, kata, genchi genbutsu, hoshin, and han-sei. Over time, the store adopted an entirely new operating philosophy, and by doing so, reaped the rewards of growth and profit.

Working from home gave Andy more time with the family, which had always been a vitally important part of his life. He was there in the morning to see everyone off to school, which he had never been able to do before—he had always been the first one out the door.

Lizzy's referral from his early days at Mainstreet Motors, the assistant principal of Twin Falls Jr./Sr. High School, eventually paid off, which opened yet another avenue for Andy to build his clientele. The teachers helped Andy design a "New Owner Workshop," which became a popular monthly seminar held in the high school multipurpose room. Soon he was handling the automobile business for the entire staff.

With every new connection, the opportunities seemed to multiply exponentially. It seemed effortless. Andy was invited to functions of all kinds. Selling a new car at a church social wasn't unheard of!

The farming market was even deeper and broader than Andy had originally thought. Everyone knew someone who needed some type of vehicle, or two or three. Kids needed cars, and Andy became the only one to buy from.

Andy was the man to trust. Word spread to other towns, and Andy's business kept growing.

Over the course of the following year, Andy found himself transformed into a highly respected advisory resource in the Twin Falls community. When you needed anything, you asked Andy, because even if he didn't know the immediate answer or solution, he knew who you had to talk to.

> I am done with great things and big plans, great institutions and big successes. I am for those tiny, invisible loving human forces that work from individual to individual, creeping through the crannies of the world like so many rootlets, or like the capillary oozing of water, yet which, if given time, will rend the hardest monuments of human pride.
>
> —WILLIAM JAMES

With Lizzy's constant prodding, Andy became a regular fixture in Mariko's Wednesday evening adult yoga class. Although at first it was difficult, Andy eventually willed himself to set aside thirty minutes each day to meditate. It became a new kata, and he added his mantra to his practice. When the weather was good and the house empty, you could find Andy outside on the deck, quieting his mind.

Mariko and Axel had given Andy a small niwa in a box, complete with tools with which to compose his Zen garden. Each weekend, Andy would spend time reconfiguring his niwa, and practicing the shibumi seven to keep them fresh in his mind: Kanso, simplicity. Koko, austerity. Seijaku, quietude. Fukinsei, asymmetry. Datsuzoku, break from convention. Shizen, naturalness. Yugen, subtlety.

One year to the day from his Mega Box termination, Andy found himself staring into the mirror as he prepared for his morning. He liked what he saw. He was proud of his commitment. He was grateful to Mainstreet Motors for giving him a chance and the means to prepare himself for a new career. His struggles and initial failures made him appreciate his accomplishment even more.

The transformation was well under way. He had come full circle to a new and better life. He had created meaningful change. Looking back, it all seemed so simple, so fitting. Lizzy and Mariko agreed that Andy had achieved a wonderful kyosei, a rare and harmonious balance. Each day brought him closer to shibumi.

As he entered the den to retrieve his briefcase, he felt a strange sensation, almost as if someone were watching him. Glancing around, his gaze came to rest upon the Daruma doll. In an instant, Andy knew what to do.

Downstairs and out to the garage and over to the workbench he raced, Daruma doll in hand. It took a minute, but he found the old jar of model paint and the brush he had used a year ago. Carefully, to match his previous work, Andy painted in the other eye of the Daruma doll.

Stepping back to appraise the finished doll in his study, he reflected on just how far he had come in one short year, and a sense of achievement and good fortune came over him. He had indeed fulfilled the promise of the doll. The thought suddenly hit him that he had only just begun the journey to shibumi. He picked up his car keys, left the house, and drove straight to The Dojo.

Andy was ready to take another step, and he needed to see Mariko about getting a new Daruma doll.

There is a vitality, a life force, an energy, a quickening that is translated through you into action, and because there is only one of you in all of time, this expression is unique. And if you block it, it will never exist through any other medium and it will be lost. The world will not have it. It is not your business to determine how good it is nor how valuable nor how it compares with other expressions. It is your business to keep it yours clearly and directly, to keep the channel open.

—MARTHA GRAHAM

the
practicum

note to reader

The Shibumi Strategy is a little story about a big breakthrough. The word itself implies the breaking of, or with, something—a mind-set, a routine, a course of action. And it has taken me the better part of adulthood to understand that breakthroughs of any kind require something to break through—an obstacle, problem, or challenge that launches a rather heroic journey, the steps of which roughly follow the chapters in the story: commitment, preparation, struggle, breakthrough, transformation.

As in the story, many times it is the involuntary challenge, the setbacks, that harbor the power to transform. The challenges that are thrown at us are generally more powerful than those we set ourselves, because most of our perceived limits are self-imposed, so our true potential isn't fully tapped no matter how high we set our goals. A sudden, unexpected crucible is a tougher test, forcing us in new directions, directions we perhaps should have taken anyway had we been more attuned, but new directions nonetheless. Approached as an opportunity—no easy task when simple survival is the first order of business—these unforeseen trials can sometimes result in an altogether new lease on life.

It is during these times of transition that we are perhaps most introspective, reflective, and receptive to the signs that might point us toward a better path. With a certain urgency, we begin to ask questions of our circumstances (Why is this happening to me?), of ourselves (What am I going to do?), and of our outcomes (Why isn't my plan working?).

Thus the lessons of *The Shibumi Strategy* come not in the form of answers but of questions. It is in the process of how we address these questions that we awaken, and we gain a degree of clarity never before experienced. To aid that process, I have included a few hansei (reflection) questions and a handful of exercises to guide a short exploration of some of the shibumi concepts and practices. I have also included some resources should you wish to explore further.

A final thought: the scope or nature of any particular breakthrough is quite irrelevant. Not every breakthrough is as life altering as the one in *The Shibumi Strategy*. And they need not be. It is the cumulative effect over one's life that is important. Make no mistake, minor tremors can have as much impact in one's life as major earthquakes. Too, they are far more prevalent and less disruptive, which is a good thing. The point is not necessarily to seek quantum leaps or dramatic shifts in direction, but to keep our senses keenly attuned to the everyday opportunities for breakthroughs that might precipitate the kind of awakening that, when all is said and done, allows us to create meaningful change.

This last concept, that of creating meaningful change, is how I think about leadership, be it personal or professional. It is a simple definition taught to me by a long-ago mentor, one that I find eminently accessible and relevant and immortal and most closely aligned to shibumi. To create is the act of bringing into existence something that was not there before. Action that is meaningful connects us to something larger, outside of ourselves, in service of others. And in that context, to change is the act of producing something new, different, and better.

All of this becomes important because at some point in life, whether our work is parenting or presiding, each of us will reflect on the most important question of all: *Have I made the most of what I have to offer the world?*

There should be only one right answer.

reflections on shibumi

Use these questions to guide the discovery of your own path to shibumi.

The Commitment
- ❏ What is the reality of my situation—dangers and opportunities?
- ❏ What am I avoiding?
- ❏ What thoughts are holding me back?
- ❏ What must I commit to?
- ❏ What am I really trying to accomplish?

The Preparation
- ❏ What specific objectives support my commitment? What is the order of priority?
- ❏ What must be accomplished? When must it be completed?
- ❏ What are my plans and strategies for meeting my objectives?

❏ What kind of assistance and support will I need from others?

❏ What are the likely obstacles? What is "plan B"?

The Struggle

❏ What are the hardest tests I face? What barriers block my way? What am I struggling with most?

❏ Which of my activities steal my energy without return? In what areas of my life and work does "try harder" fail? What happens when I "try easy" instead?

❏ What can I simplify? How can I exploit or better manage complexity in my life?

❏ What can I eliminate, reduce, or subtract to make more room for what matters most? What would those who matter most to me love for me to stop doing?

❏ What can I leave unfinished without loss of impact? What might I leave incomplete, uncertain, or ambiguous that would create curiosity and engagement in those viewing my work?

The Breakthrough

❏ What is the "why not?" in my field? The "what if?"

❏ What rules, routines, and regimens seem limiting?

❏ How can I use those limitations to spark new ways of thinking?

❏ What can I do to take a physical or mental break from what I'm struggling with?

❏ What new rules can I develop? What new standards?

The Transformation

❏ Who am I helping to succeed? What do they need most from me?

❏ What new ways of thinking and acting are needed to sustain the change I've made? How will I deepen them?

❏ What new perceptions, values, and experiences will be critical to my continued success?

❏ What opportunities exist to further strengthen the new direction? How will I capitalize on them?

❏ In what areas can I improve the most? What areas require rebalancing?

kata for practice

Use the short exercises and templates in this short tutorial to develop routines for the key practices:

- Genchi genbutsu (observation)
- Hoshin (goal alignment)
- Kaizen (continuous improvement)
- Hansei (reflection)

GENCHI GENBUTSU

Genchi genbutsu (go look, go see) is the key to shibumi in solving problems and feeding opportunities. Detectives are masters in the art of observation. In fact, since the 1920s, the New York Police Department (NYPD) has focused on the power of observation in screening and training police officers, using art as the tool. The public domain sketch from the New York State Civil Service Commission on the next page was given to officer candidates for three minutes, during which time note-taking

was allowed. They were then given ten minutes to answer ten questions. The goal was to identify and select in advance those with a natural talent for grasping and intelligently perceiving what is right in front of them. Then-Commissioner William Gorham Rice wrote, "Many men have eyes but they do not see." Not only was the test effective for identifying candidates with a natural ability to fix in mind the facts that a police officer should see, it also successfully indicated those most likely to overlook the more significant facts in any situation.

Try it for yourself: gaze at the picture for three minutes, taking notes if you wish. Cover the picture, then try to answer these questions:

- What is the number of the policeman's badge?
- What is the condition of the weather?
- What railway line operates the trolley car?
- Assuming this accident occurred in the daytime, did it occur in the morning or the afternoon? (Why?)
- On what street was the automobile being driven?
- What is the date of the accident?
- What was the registration number of the automobile?

143

- What is the last name of the person to whom the automobile is probably registered?
- What two things indicate that the chauffeur was killed, not merely injured?
- What shows reckless driving on the part of the chauffeur?

To this day, the NYPD trains new detectives using art. Training is conducted on Mondays at the Frick Collection on East 70th Street in Manhattan, when the museum is closed. Detectives are taught a kata that allows them to arrive at the who, what, where, why, and when of a painting. The process begins with observation and description, moving from foreground to background, followed by analysis and conclusion. The result is a better perspective in the field at an actual crime scene.

Whether it's a painting or a real-life situation, here is the kata:

1. *Describe*. Record the facts, and just the facts, of the situation. Scrutinize and describe in detail what you see and what is known. Refrain from interpreting or concluding.

144

2. *Inquire.* Ask and answer the who, what, where, when, how, and why of the situation.
3. *Conclude.* Based on your description and inquiry, use your notes to draw conclusions, framing problems and outlining opportunities.

HOSHIN

The goal of hoshin is to create a framework for transparent direction and strategic alignment. Everyone with a stake in your sphere of performance should be aware of, and have input to, your direction, goals and activities. A simple template works well to frame the kata of hoshin.

For example, if your intent is to "grow my business in harmony with my partners," you might think about using the following framework, sharing it and gaining feedback from all those who have a stake in your vision, then adjusting things based on that input.

Direction or Goal	Key Initiative	Key Activity	Key Targets	Key Measure	Assignment	Timing	Budget
1.							
2.							
3.							

KAIZEN

The kata of kaizen may be thought of as an endless repetition of three steps:

1. Create a standard (a kata!).
2. Follow it.
3. Find a better way.

What drives kaizen is a cycle of constant improvement and creative problem solving, conducted in an experimental, iterative loop, the acronym for which is IDEA:

Investigate. Using genchi genbutsu, conduct fact finding needed to fully assess and analyze the situation, challenge, problem, or opportunity.
❏ What are you trying to achieve, and why is it important?
❏ What are the facts and issues?
❏ Why is the situation the way it is?

Design. Using the shibumi seven principles (kanso, koko, seijaku, shizen, fukinsei, datsuzoku, yugen), generate ideas and solutions based on the complete investigation.

❏ What are the possibilities for the ideal state?

❏ What ideas, options, and alternatives exist for achieving it?

❏ What is the chosen direction forward?

Execution. Using hoshin planning basics, conduct an experiment to quickly test a solution or design prototype.

❏ What do you expect will happen?

❏ What is the intended scope of impact or gain?

❏ What tasks, targets, measures, timing, and assignment will let you test the idea?

Adjustment. Using hansei, assess results and improve the design based on the gap between what was expected and what occurred.

❏ What is the gap between expectation and outcome?

❏ What accounts for the difference, if any?

❏ What adjustments and next steps must be made?

HANSEI

Hansei (reflection, introspection) can range from open-ended introspection such as the questions in the "Reflections on Shibumi" section to the tactical U.S. Army after-action review (AAR) process. Hansei is a significant part of achieving mastery, as the fruit of hansei is new insights that can be used to set new goals, strategies, and directions.

The late Peter Drucker, in his 1999 book *Management Challenges for the Twenty-First Century*, suggested a practical reflection method that amounts to a daily routine of recording in a personal journal your key decisions and actions, along with a projection of the expected outcome. You then review your performance and satisfaction—comparing outcomes to expectations. He suggested getting additional input from a superior, peer, or subordinate. Over time, trends show up that point out strengths and weaknesses. Drucker wrote, "I have been doing this for some fifteen to twenty years now. And every time I do it, I am surprised. And so is everyone who has ever done this."

In their 2001 book *Now, Discover Your Strengths*, Marcus Buckingham and Donald Clifton echo Drucker's recommendation, stating, "Probably the best way to pinpoint your talents is to monitor your behavior and your feelings over an extended period of time."

I have a simple hansei regimen that I look forward to each day. It has a bit of both worlds, and it has definitely yielded some surprises in the form of both good and what prove to be not-so-good ideas.

Here's what to do:

1. *Make time.* Try to set aside at least fifteen minutes per day to start. But don't be limited either way . . . if you only have five minutes, use it. If you're on a roll, don't stop.

2. *Review experience.* Use the AAR technique to answer three simple questions as they relate to your day: What was supposed to happen? What actually happened? What accounts for any differences or gaps between what you planned or expected to happen and what actually happened?

3. *Spot trends.* As time progresses and you've done this for a while, note any recurring themes, and write down any potential connections among seemingly unconnected things.

4. *Riff and project.* Think of a few what-if ideas that come to mind based on the first three steps. Jot down opportunities that could test those

new ideas. Take your what-ifs and turn them into "if-then" hypotheses: What do you think will happen if you do X? Make some quick notes—to-do items, not-to-do items, and so on—that will initiate your thoughts and provide some preliminary direction.

Hansei is meant to help you improve your performance and creativity by getting your thoughts and actions better aligned by making them more visible to yourself. The hardest part, of course, is step one.

I suggest using a journal. The art of journaling is centuries old. Leonardo da Vinci's notebooks and journals, which capture his thoughts, advice, and inventions, are world renowned. It is reported that Apple's Steve Jobs paid millions of dollars for a single original page.

A suggestion: It helps if you don't view reflection as a chore or reflective journaling as a strict linear writing exercise. So you might want to avoid using a lined journal and consider a blank-page Moleskine (available at moleskineus.com) or my favorite, the design-award–winning Muji Chronotebook Nonlinear Planner (available at muji.com).

notes and references

THE PREPARATION

You can read more about Daruma at http://www.onmark-productions.com/html/daruma.shtml, and more about the Daruma doll at http://en.wikipedia.org/wiki/Daruma_doll. Access date: April 29, 2010.

. . . science to what Mariko told us about kaizen: Dr. Robert Maurer, a psychologist on the staff at the UCLA medical school, discusses the neuroscience of change in *One Small Step Can Change Your Life: The Kaizen Way* (New York: Workman, 2004).

THE STRUGGLE

After-action review: The best source for further reading on After Action Reviews is in *Be-Know-Do, Adapted from the Official Army Leadership Manual: Leadership the Army Way,* by Richard Cavanagh (Jossey-Bass, 2004).

Lao Tzu . . . Tao Te Ching: The verse by Chinese philosopher Lao Tzu can be found in his *Tao Te Ching,* trans. Gia-Fu Feng and Jane English (New York: Vintage Books, 1989), chapter 11.

. . . Olympic team in the late 1980s: This story can be found in *If It Ain't Broke . . . Break It: And Other Unconventional Wisdom for a Changing Business World*, by Robert Kriegel and Louis Palter (New York: Warner Business Books, 1992).

This one's about a fly: This story is from psychologist Price Pritchett, and can be found in *Chicken Soup for the Soul*, edited by Jack Canfield and Mark Victor Hansen (Deerfield Beach, Fla.: Health Communications, 1993).

Sfumato: A discussion of *sfumato* can be found in *The Story of Art*, 16th ed., by E. H. Gombrich (London: Phaidon Press, 1995), and "Blurred Images and the Unvarnished Truth," *British Journal of Aesthetics* 2 (1962), pp. 170–79.

THE BREAKTHROUGH

There are several excellent discussions of the Eureka moment and the role of the "break": Semir Zeki, "Artistic Creativity and the Brain," *Science* 293 (July 6, 2001), pp. 51–52; Guenther Knoblich and Michael Oellinger, "The Eureka Moment," *Scientific American Mind* 17, no. 5 (2006): 38–43; Robert Stickgold and others, "Visual Discrimination Learning Requires Sleep After Training," *Nature Neuroscience* 13, no. 12 (December 2000): 1237–1238; Ullrich Wagner and others, "Sleep Inspires Insight," *Nature* 427 (January 22, 2004): 352–355; and Robert Stickgold and Jeffrey Ellenbogen, "Quiet! Sleeping Brain at Work," *Scientific American Mind* 19, no. 4 (August/September 2008): 22–29.

It was a whole four-year study: The discussion of the consulting firm experiment can be found in "Making Time Off Predictable—And Required," by Leslie A. Perlow and Jessica L. Porter, *Harvard Business Review* (October 2009).

. . . Buddhist monks are among the most studied groups: Sharon Begley, science editor for *Newsweek* and former *Wall Street Journal* science columnist, has written extensively on the studies of Tibetan monks: *Train Your Mind, Change Your Brain* (New York: Ballantine Books, 2007); "How Thinking Can Change the Brain," *Wall Street Journal*, January 19, 2007; and "Scans of Monks' Brains Show Meditation Alters Structure, Functioning," *Wall Street Journal*, November 5, 2004.

DARUMA DOLLS

Daruma dolls are available from a number of Web sites, including

- Wishingfish.com
- Mrslinskitchen.com
- Welovedaruma.com
- Jun-gifts.com

glossary

JAPANESE

Datsuzoku: Break from routine or habit or convention, surprise

Fukinsei: Asymmetry, beautiful imperfection

Genchi genbutsu: "Go look, go see," observation

Hansei: Reflection, introspection

Hoshin: Goal alignment; strategic plan

Kaizen: Continuous improvement

Kanso: Simplicity

Kata: Routine, basic form

Kiki: Crisis, "danger and opportunity"

Koko: Austerity

Kyosei: Balance, harmony borne of opposing tensions

Niwa: Friendship garden

Seijaku: Quietude, stillness

Shibumi: Elegant simplicity, effortless effectiveness, understated beauty

Shizen: Naturalness, authenticity, being without pretense

Yugen: Subtlety

ITALIAN

Sfumato: "Like smoke," smoky, blurry, ambiguous, uncertain

Sprezzatura: Art of making difficult things look easy

reading and resources

Here I have included some of my favorite books and articles—a blend of both Eastern and Western art, philosophy, design, and science—should you wish to explore the Zen of shibumi further in a variety of contexts.

BOOKS

Sharon Begley, *Train Your Mind, Change Your Brain: How a New Science Reveals Our Extraordinary Power to Transform Ourselves* (New York: Ballantine Books, 2007).

David Chalmers, *The Conscious Mind: In Search of a Fundamental Theory* (Oxford, England: Oxford University Press, 1997).

Matthew Crawford, *Shop Class as Soulcraft* (New York: Penguin Books, 2009).

Masaaki Imai, *Kaizen* (New York: McGraw-Hill/Irwin, 1986).

Ellen J. Langer, *Mindfulness* (Reading, Mass.: Addison-Wesley, 1990).

Robert Pirsig, *Zen and the Art of Motorcycle Maintenance* (New York: Morrow, 1974).

Michael Ray and Rochelle Myers, *Creativity in Business* (New York: Doubleday, 1986).

Garr Reynolds, *Presentation Zen* (Berkeley, Calif.: New Riders Press, 2008).

Jeffrey Schwartz, *Brain Lock* (New York: HarperCollins, 1996).

Jeffrey M. Schwartz and Sharon Begley, *The Mind and the Brain: Neuroplasticity and the Power of Mental Force* (New York: Regan Books, 2003).

Trevanian, *Shibumi* (New York: Crown, 1979).

ARTICLES

Ann Emmert Abbott, "The Value of Idle Hours," *Artist's Sketchbook* (Oct. 2004).

Warren Bennis and Robert Thomas, "Crucibles of Leadership," *Harvard Business Review* (Sept. 2002).

Robert Epstein, "The Dalai Lama on. . . . The Science of Meditation," *Psychology Today* (June 2001).

Guenther Knoblich and Michael Oellinger, "The Eureka Moment," *Scientific American Mind* 17, no. 5 (2006).

Ulrich Kraft, "Unleashing Creativity," *Scientific American Mind* 16, no. 1 (2005).

D. T. Max, "Wired for Victory," *Men's Vogue* (Jan./Feb. 2007).

Steven Pinker and others, "The Brain: A User's Guide," *Time Magazine Mind & Body Special Issue* 169, no. 5 (2007).

Lennox Tierney, "The Nature of Japanese Garden Art," n.d. Available at http://niwa.org/philosophy. Access date Apr. 15, 2010.

Ullrich Wagner and others, "Sleep Inspires Insight," *Nature* 427 (Jan. 22, 2004).

Semir Zeki, "Artistic Creativity and the Brain," *Science* 293 (July 6, 2001).

about the author

Matthew E. May is an internationally recognized expert on innovation and design strategy. He has been featured by the *Wall Street Journal*, CNN, and National Public Radio. He is a columnist for the American Express Small Business OPEN Forum Idea Hub where he writes in the popular "The World" section. He is the author most recently of *In Pursuit of Elegance* (2009), which was named to *Business Week*'s 2009 Best Business Books in the Design/Innovation category. His preceding book, *The Elegant Solution* (2006), won the Shingo Research Prize for Excellence. A popular speaker and adviser in design thinking, Matt lectures to more than fifty corporations, governments, and universities around the world each year, and works confidentially with creative teams and senior leaders at a number of Fortune-listed companies. His articles have appeared in national publications such as *USA Today, Design Mind, Strategy & Business*, and *MIT/Sloan Management Review*.

Matt is a graduate of the Wharton School and the Johns Hopkins University, but considers winning the *New Yorker* Cartoon Caption Contest among his proudest achievements.

The Shibumi Strategy is his first fable.